# TITUS
## Patterns for
## Church Living

# James T. Draper, Jr.

# TITUS

## Patterns for Church Living

Tyndale House
Publishers, Inc.
Wheaton, Illinois

Scripture quotations are taken
from the King James Version
except where otherwise indicated.
Those marked TLB are taken
from *The Living Bible* (© 1971 by
Tyndale House Publishers).

Library of Congress Catalog Card
Number 77-93758.
ISBN 0-8423-7225-3.
Copyright © 1978 by James T.
Draper, Jr.
First printing, May, 1978.
Printed in the United States of
America.

# CONTENTS

It is the great desire in the heart of God that his people be united in purpose and faithful in the ministry committed to them through the local church. Any disorder or dissension is an affront to God and a detriment to the purposes of our Lord Jesus Christ.

These pages are a simple exposition of Paul's instructions to Titus concerning the churches in Crete. Disorder, confusion, and heresy reigned supreme on that beautiful island. Titus was sent to bring order out of the chaos and unity out of the divisions.

Each passage should be read before studying the chapters in this book. As you read these pages, do so with your Bible open and your heart in prayer for God's illumination. May these studies prove to be as profitable to you as they have been to our hearts here in God's church in Euless.

# The Hope of Eternal Life
## *Titus 1:1-4*

NEXT TO TIMOTHY, Titus was probably the most cherished, the most confidential friend that the Apostle Paul had. Paul mentioned the young Christian servant in 2 Corinthians and in Galatians. Though Titus does not appear in the book of Acts, a history of the early church, we do know a great deal about him.

Titus was converted under the ministry of the Apostle Paul, then became a very close associate of the great apostle. Paul sent Titus to Corinth to deliver 1 Corinthians. Then Titus met Paul in Macedonia and reported on the progress of the work in Corinth. Paul then sat down and penned 2 Corinthians as a result of what Titus shared with him. Titus was a trusted associate and a valued ally. He was not Jewish by birth, but was a Greek.

Paul sent Titus to the island of Crete to establish order in the churches there. We do not know how these churches began, but many believe they were a direct result of the Day of Pentecost. New converts from that day may well have established Christian churches in Crete. When Judaizers, false teachers, began teaching the Cretans that law-keeping is necessary for salvation, the churches were in an uproar. Paul's letter gave Titus instructions on how to straighten out the situation.

The express mission of Titus is recorded in these words: "I left you there on the island of Crete so that you could do whatever was needed to help strengthen each of its churches, and I asked you to appoint pastors in every city who would follow the instructions I gave you" (1:5, TLB). Titus was to appoint pastors who would be true to the divine purposes of redemption and declare the truth.

Before going into the qualifications of spiritual leadership, let's take a good look at the opening verses of Titus.

A CALLING RECEIVED

"Paul, a servant of God, and an apostle of Jesus Christ . . ." (1:1). The casual Bible student would read that and say, "Let's go on to the important things." But this greeting reveals part of the heart of the Christian faith.

The word "apostle" means "one who has the command and the authority to act in behalf of another." In our day, we might call it the power of attorney. Paul said, "I am representing Jesus Christ. I am sent forth as his personal emissary to the world." The sooner we realize that we have been commissioned to be personal representatives of Jesus Christ to our world, the sooner we will minister as God wants us to minister. Though we are not exactly apostles, we too have a divine assignment.

This preaching of the gospel "is committed unto me

according to the commandment of God our Saviour" (1:3). Paul declared, "I am not preaching and ministering to you because I decided that is what I wanted to do. God commanded me to do it. I stand as his representative." In our day and our time we, too, must stand as called ones of God, called to present Jesus Christ to a lost world.

Paul also considered himself "a servant of God." The Greek word for "servant" is a very common Greek word referring to the most abject, servile person, literally meaning "slave." He declared, "I am a slave of God." To follow Jesus Christ means we become a slave to him, we sell out totally to him. "Ye are not your own. For ye are bought with a price" (1 Corinthians 6:19, 20).

This word "slave" has four possible meanings. First of all, it could represent one who is born into slavery. By his first birth, the Apostle Paul was born a slave of sin. He was born with a nature that drew back from God, that resisted God, that rebelled against God. When he was reborn into God's family, he was again born into slavery, slavery to Jesus Christ. That is true of every child of God. Every believer is a slave by rebirth.

The word "slave" can also refer to one who is bound so tightly to his master that only death can break the bonds. When the believer died with Jesus Christ (Galatians 2:20), he stopped being a slave to Satan because death freed him. When Paul declared in Romans 6:3, "Know ye not, that so many of us as were baptized into Jesus Christ were baptized into his death?" he was declaring for all of us who belong to God that by death we have been freed from sin, we have been released from slavery to Satan, and we have received the life of Christ. Since Christ never dies, our bondage to him never ceases. Our service is eternal and will never cease. It transcends time. Our bonds to sin are broken by the death of Christ. Our new life binds us with ties that shall never be broken.

"Slave" also refers to one whose will is lost in the will of another. Before he was saved, the Apostle Paul did what Satan wanted him to do. The first chapters of Acts record the vile and ungodly deeds. When he came to God and received new life, his will was lost in the sweet will of God. That is what it means to be a slave of God. We have no will of our own, no rights of our own. We belong to him. His will is our will. His wish is our command.

The word "slave" can also mean "one who serves another with complete disregard for himself." Anyone who has ever served Satan would have to be honest enough to say he did not do it unselfishly. Even worse, when one does what Satan wants him to do, Satan always cheats him, lies to him, deceives him. When one serves Satan, he is serving against his own best interests.

When the Apostle Paul became a slave to God, he began a new life, with complete disregard for his own safety and purposes. When he was accused by the Jews, he could have stayed in Jerusalem and have been acquitted. But because he knew that God wanted him in Rome, he appealed to Caesar. "Fear not, Paul; thou must be brought before Caesar" (Acts 27:24 KJV). It was in the interest of God's kingdom that he went to Rome, not his own. He was a slave.

The wonderful truth is that whatever is in the best interest of God is in our best interest too. Real joy and real happiness lie in doing God's will. As we learn to serve

God unselfishly, we learn that being a Christian is not just a way of coming to church on Sunday, not just a way of praying or singing, not just a way of doing certain things, but the best way of doing everything. We see in God's calling a description of what we are to be. Our hearts, our lives, all that we are belongs to him. We are to be servants of God and representatives of Jesus Christ.

A CONFIDENCE RETAINED

"Paul, a servant of God, and an apostle of Jesus Christ, according to the faith of God's elect, and the acknowledging of the truth which is after godliness" (1:1). According to this verse, we have a confidence in God that is revealed in two areas. Paul declared his calling to be consistent with the truth of the Word of God and with the faith that operates in the lives of God's people.

I don't know why the translators rendered this "the acknowledging of the truth." "Acknowledging" is a noun, literally "knowledge." It means "full knowledge" or "whole knowledge." Paul was simply saying that God's people should not be ignorant. That's why we study. That's why we preach and teach the Word of God. The only way we can have confidence in our warfare with the world, the only way we can cope with the complex problems we face is to possess a full and complete knowledge of the truth of the Word of God.

Faith comes by hearing and hearing by the Word of God (Romans 10:17). God's answer to doubt, despair, discouragement, and depression is confidence, confidence through the knowledge of the Word of God. "My apostleship, my servitude, is consistent with the full knowledge God has given me," said Paul.

### A CANDOR REQUIRED

"So that they can have eternal life, which God promised them before the world began—he cannot lie" (1:2, TLB). If God is not a God of candor, honesty, integrity, we have no hope. If God does not keep his Word, if his integrity is not beyond reproach, we have nothing upon which to stand.

Many churches discuss theology, philosophy, and logic, but they're inconclusive, incomplete, with no "Thus saith the Lord" to point them to solid ground. Unless there is a God who doesn't stammer and who means what he says, there is no hope. Someone said, "God said it, I believe it, and that settles it." That is true, but not the entire truth. God said it and that settles it, whether or not I believe it! God cannot lie.

The little phrase "cannot lie" is the Greek word *apseudes*. A pseudonym is a false name, an assumed name. The *a* in the Greek language reverses the meaning of the word. He is a God without falsehood. He always tells the truth. Our salvation is not based on our emotions or feelings, but upon the fact that God, who cannot lie, has promised in his Word to save those who come in repentance and faith to him.

I can tell you without question that I am saved, because I know there was a time in my life when I turned from my sin and turned to God. When I received him, he saved me. I know it. I do not have to be torn by doubt because my salvation does not depend on my integrity; it depends on God's.

A CONCEALMENT REMOVED

"And now in his own good time he has revealed this Good News and permits me to tell it to everyone" (1:3, TLB). The words "in his own good time" simply mean that at a time of God's choosing, he revealed his gospel through preaching. We need to be reminded often that every aspect of our relationship to God is based upon God's initiative. We would have no desire to be saved and we would have no desire to serve God if God the Holy Spirit did not deal with us in our hearts.

Adam hid from God, and the Scriptures picture God as seeking for him. It has been that way ever since. God is calling for man, but always in God's time. "Now is the accepted time" (2 Corinthians 6:2). Now is the time when we are to be saved, says God. Now is the time when we are to respond to him. When we feel the touch of God upon our lives, when we feel the movement of the Holy Spirit in our hearts, we should cherish that conviction. We must water it with our tears and with our repentance. We must respond now.

In due time, God's Good News was revealed. The word "revealed" means to unveil something that was hidden. The gospel had been hidden; people didn't understand it. But in God's time, he explained it to them.

Eternal truth was revealed in God's time—"through preaching" (KJV). That is why preaching ought to be based upon the Word of God. Preaching God's message is his method of revealing hidden truth. Preaching should reveal God. It should declare his intents and purposes.

God wants us to know eternal truth. God wants us to walk hand in hand in fellowship with him. He wants to live in us and walk beside us. He wants to live his life through us. He wants to love a world through us. That is God's intent, and it needs to be revealed.

Some of us may have been in church for years and never realized that God wanted to use us as instruments to reach out to our families and to this lost world with the gospel. God help us to proclaim and display his truth.

A COMMUNITY REVEALED

"To Titus, mine own son after the common faith..." (1:4). The word "common" is the Greek word *koine*. The New Testament was written in what is called *koine* Greek, common Greek, everyday language. The New Testament was not written in classical Greek, the language of literature, or the words of the philosophers. It was written in the common language so everyone could understand it. That is the word used here to describe our faith.

Paul said, "Titus is my son after a common faith." Titus was a Greek, Paul a Jew. But Paul was saying, "We have a common faith. God loves us both. God has a purpose for both of us. God has a common desire for our lives and hearts." God's community is for everyone. His is a universal message, one that all can understand, one that all desperately need. It is good for rich and poor, young and old, black and white, educated and unlearned, men of all races, creeds, and nationalities.

That is the message of the Word of God. None of us are left outside of it. None of us are too insignificant to be touched by it. None of us are too untalented to be used in the community of the faith. That is the good news of the gospel. God loves every one of us. He calls us to salvation and to service. He gives us a confidence upon which to base that relationship, even the confidence of the full knowledge of the truth as revealed in his Word.

He backs it up with an integrity that is unquestionable. God is not capable of lying. We know that he stands upon his Word. What a beautiful gospel that was in that day, and it has not lost any of its beauty, for it is the same today. It is the gospel of salvation. It is the message the world desperately needs. It is a message of love in a world of hate, a message of light in a world of darkness, a message of truth in a world of lies and falsehoods. That is the message God has entrusted to us.

# Qualifications for Leadership
## *Titus 1:5-9*

THERE ARE TWO SIGNIFICANT things God says to us through this passage of Scripture. First, we have every right to know what we should expect from our pastor ("elder," KJV). And since God spells it out, we can know what to expect. By the way, the churches in Crete evidently had no deacons, as Paul's instructions to Titus did not mention the appointing of deacons. That is probably because the churches were so young and immature that the bishops or pastors were to perform all the functions of both pastors and deacons. The qualities here can and should be applied to deacons as well as pastors.

Secondly, there is a special challenge to every believer here. In writing to Timothy, the great apostle declared, "Don't let anyone think little of you because you are young. Be their ideal; let them follow the way you teach and live; be a pattern for them in your love, your faith, and your clean thoughts" (1 Timothy 4:12, TLB). That means we are to set the example, the pattern. It is important for us to have godly leaders in the church because they will show us what we ought to be. If a man says he belongs to Christ, he is to walk even as Jesus walked (1 John 2:6). Jesus revealed a certain kind of conduct, character, and godliness, modeling what God wants me to be. Similarly, our leaders are to so show us how to live, giving us an example by which we can grow and mature into the very likeness of Christ.

THE PATTERN FOR THE CHURCH

What is God's desire for the church? "For this cause left I thee in Crete, that thou shouldest set in order the things that are wanting, and ordain elders in every city, as I had appointed thee" (1:5). The phrase "set in order" is a medical term which means to correct something that has been broken; e.g., a broken bone. God sent Titus to bring proper perspective to the churches.

It is important for us to understand the problems that Titus faced. Titus was instructed to go to the island of Crete and organize the churches, to dispel any disorder or confusion. He was to ordain elders or pastors in the churches. This was a very critical mission because the churches already had pastors, and a semblance of organization. Apparently these pastors were not doctrinally sound, were not the kind of men who should be leading. Titus was to go into the chaos, confusion, and disorganization and produce order. Dismissing the unqualified pastors and appointing good ones would not be easy.

God does not want the church confused or disorganized. He does not want contention in the church. He wants the church to operate smoothly. He wants the church organized for its best effort. False doctrine, confusion, and error always disgust God. Rather, he wants godliness and true spirituality to unite his people.

The church at Corinth faced similar confusion. They were even baptizing for the dead, a pagan practice. In the midst of his discussion of the gifts of the Holy Spirit, the Apostle Paul made a very clear statement about the intent of God for the church: "God is not one who likes things to be disorderly and upset. He likes harmony, and he finds it in all the other churches. . . . However, be sure that everything is done properly in a good and orderly way" (1 Corinthians 14:33, 40, TLB).

Anything that brings disorder is a threat to the church. Even doctrine can be a point of contention. It is possible for us to stand so firmly for the truth (as we understand it) that we do it in a wrong way, with a vindictive, divisive, bitter spirit. It isn't wrong to disagree, but it is wrong to be disagreeable. God's people were never intended to divide over doctrine (or anything else). Certainly we are not going to always agree, but there ought to be an order and a peace in our fellowship in the church. That is what Paul was instructing Titus. "In Crete there is chaos. You go set it straight. Bring the churches and the people together in a common purpose."

Suppose that we go out to a beautiful lake for a picnic. There is a long pier that goes out into the lake, and some people are fishing from that pier. Children are running back and forth when suddenly a section of the pier collapses, and some of our children who cannot swim fall into the lake. Suppose that our first reaction was to open discussion on the pros and cons of building a better pier since this one is obviously too dangerous. The children are going under for the third time, and we're discussing whether or not we need a new pier! It just needs to be shored up, says one man. Someone else suggests that it just needs painting. A new color would make all the difference in the world. And while we spend our time discussing the necessity for changing or renovating the pier, the children drown!

That is a ridiculous illustration, but that is exactly what the modern church is doing. There is too much at stake for us to major on minors. Dare we waste time and effort through disorder and disorganization while those around us are dying? God deplores disorder, so he sent Titus to set in order the things that were lacking.

THE PATTERN FOR CHURCH LEADERSHIP

A second part of the pattern for the church is the ordination or appointing of elders. The word "elders" (KJV) can be translated "bishop" or "pastor." The church is a divine institution, and God planned that men of God would lead the church. This does not mean that the people in the church have no voice, but the church is not a pure democracy. It is a theocracy, a government under God. The people are led by the men of God whom God has placed over them. The pastor has a responsibility under God that must not be discarded. He must be the spearhead for what God is doing.

The writer of Hebrews declared, "Remember your leaders who have taught you the Word of God. Think of all the good that has come from their lives, and try to trust the Lord as they do. . . . Obey your spiritual leaders and be willing to do what they say. For their work is to watch over your souls, and God will judge them on how well they do this. Give them reason to report joyfully about you to the Lord and not with sorrow, for then you will suffer for it too" (Hebrews 13:7, 17, TLB). Are ordained men to be dictatorial? Not at all! However, they have a responsibility under God to lead. Without someone to lead or make binding decisions, we would spend all of our time discussing and not doing. There has to be some authority placed by God in the church. The pastorate is a sacred trust. God says in effect, "You are responsible to lead my people. If one of these little ones falls by the wayside because of your neglect, you must answer to me."

Furthermore, "the men you choose must be well thought of for their good lives; they must have only one wife and their children must love the Lord and not have a reputation for being wild or disobedient to their parents" (1:6, TLB). Being "well thought of" means that he is a man one would not dare accuse of anything wrong. The King James Version translates this "blameless." An ordained man in the church should be a man who cannot be charged with wrongdoing. He is a man whose life stands behind what he preaches. He is a man of honesty, character, integrity, and morality. It must be so for all to see.

This blamelessness expresses itself in three areas. First of all, it involves *his family*. He is to have only one wife. In the Greek that literally means "one woman man."

That is not to say that an ordained man has to be married. Polygamy was a real problem in Paul's day. The pastor cannot have more than one wife. He must be blameless in his home.

The apostle continued by emphasizing that the pastor is to have faithful children (literally, "children of the faith" or "believing children"). He is to be a man whose children have given themselves to Jesus Christ. If a man cannot lead his own family to Christ, how can he lead other families to him?

Concerning his children, we read, "not accused of riot" (KJV). The word "riot" is the same word that Luke 15:13 uses to describe the prodigal son—he "wasted his substance with riotous living." It literally means "the inability to save" or "one who wastes his money on his own pleasure." The children of God's man must not be like that. They are, further, not to be "disobedient" (TLB). That is a term meaning that they are not to be physically uncontrollable. They are in subjection in their homes and in the community.

The pastor is also to be blameless in his *personal life*. "For a bishop must be blameless, as the steward of God, not self-willed, not soon angry, not given to wine, no striker, not given to filthy lucre; but a lover of hospitality, a lover of good men, sober, just, holy, temperate" (1:7, 8). Here is the word "blameless" again, "blameless, as the steward of God." The word "steward" is taken from two Greek words, one meaning "house" and the other meaning "law." A steward is one who administers the law whereby a house is governed. The bishop, a steward of God, is given the responsibility for administering the church, or overseeing its program and activities.

As a steward, he must not be self-willed or proud. He cannot afford to have an overgrown ego. He should not be "soon angry." This is one word in the Greek, meaning "not hotheaded." He doesn't jump to conclusions or look for a reason to fight. Further, he is "not given to wine." He is not one who uses alcoholic beverages. "No striker" is a word meaning that he does not allow his anger to move into violence. He has self-control.

"Not given to filthy lucre" means that he does not make money and material possessions his chief pursuit of life. One of the greatest tragedies that I see in Christianity today is that there are many preachers who are involved in sideline financial endeavors so that they become businessmen in addition to preachers. Their interests are divided. God does not intend for that to be. This doesn't mean that a man who leads a church can't have investments. But he must beware of being distracted from his top priority—preaching the Word of God.

On the positive side, the pastor is to be "a lover of hospitality." That is one word in the Greek and means "lover of strangers." In the first century, many Christians had been kicked out of their homes and their possessions were confiscated. Many had no place to go. In the church, they met other Christians. They were strangers, and yet were received with great hospitality by their brothers and sisters in Christ. It is easy to see how the church grew and Christianity prospered in the first century. We should welcome the stranger. Not just with a "Come over to my house and have a hamburger," but with a deep desire to help that stranger in need.

The pastor must also be "a lover of good men." The original literally means "a lover of good"—good people, good doctrine, etc. He is to love good with all of his heart. He is to be a "sober" man, which means he has his thoughts under control. He is to think clearly and precisely at all times.

He is also to be a "just" man. There are two ideas involved in this. The only way we can be just before God is to repent of our sins and give our lives to him. We must also be fair and honest in our dealings with each other. The pastor is also to be "holy." This does not mean that he is so pious that he is far above the rest of us. The word "holy" literally means "complete, whole." He is a person that is well-rounded, a man who knows where he is going. "Temperate" simply means "self-mastered." In this context, it means a man whose self has been mastered by his commitment to Christ, and thus he presents himself to the Holy Spirit for his use.

Not only is the pastor to be blameless in his family and personal life, he is to be blameless in *what he believes*. "Holding fast the faithful word as he hath been taught, that he may be able by sound doctrine both to exhort and to convince the gainsayers" (1:9).

"Holding fast" means "to hang on, to stand by." We are to hang on to proper doctrine. Our great commitment and dedication are to be to hold fast the faithful Word, the Scriptures, and to Christ, the personal Word of God. The man who stands to lead a church ought to be a man who holds on to God's written Word and God's living Word.

He is to hang on to the Word of God so he can use "sound doctrine." That combination of words literally means "healthy teachings," teachings which enable us to exhort and convince. The word "exhort" means "to plead so as to comfort and encourage," to present God's case and plead for response under the leadership of the Holy Spirit. We plead with people to commit themselves to God, to hold on to God's healthy doctrines.

When we make that kind of exhortation, we will "convince the gainsayers." The word "convince" means "to convict." When we hold the proper truth and are the kind of person God wants us to be, we will be able to exhort people in such a way that they will be convicted and will turn to him.

That is God's pattern for the church and its leadership. Not disorder, but spiritual leadership guided by the Holy Spirit. Pastors are to be the spiritual spearheads, the guides, the ones responsible for the direction that the church takes.

Combating
Heresy
*Titus 1:10-14*

FROM THE VERY BEGINNING, the Christian church has suffered under the oppressive hand of persecution. To be a Christian for many meant to give up their jobs, their properties, their families, their lives. They were hunted and hounded, driven away from their societies. However, persecution has never fatally hurt the church. Indeed, the church's greatest growth has come when the heavy hand of the enemy was upon believers. Such times seem to call for special commitment and courage. But perhaps the greatest danger to the church is false doctrine and heresy. There is a subtle tendency to work into the teachings of the church that which is not true, mixing man's ideas with God's truth. Such a mixture of human wisdom and divine wisdom forms what the Bible calls heresy.

These verses tell us what to do about heresy. "For there are many who refuse to obey; this is especially true among those who say that all Christians must obey the Jewish laws. But this is foolish talk; it blinds people to the truth, and it must be stopped. Already whole families have been turned away from the grace of God. Such teachers are only after your money. One of their own men, a prophet from Crete, has said about them, 'These men of Crete are all liars; they are like lazy animals, living only to satisfy their stomachs.' And this is true. So speak to the Christians there as sternly as necessary to make them strong in the faith, and to stop them from listening to Jewish folk tales and the demands of men who have turned their backs on the truth" (1:10-14, TLB).

The warning is very clear. We are to avoid heresy and excesses in any form. This is so applicable to us today. On one extreme, we have a misunderstanding of the ministry of the Holy Spirit and a resulting extreme emotionalism. At the other extreme, we have a pseudo-intellectualism that humanizes God and his Word and makes man's mind and intelligence to be the final authority. Heresy is no stranger to our age.

How can we deal with heresy today?

THE HERETIC DESCRIBED

False teachers tell lies as though they were the truth. They are unruly and insubordinate. Promoting heresy within the framework of the church, they refuse to accept the authority of the Word of God.

God put a divine order in the church. He gave the church his Word, the basis for all we do and say. If our interpretation or creed contradicts at any point with the Word of God, the Word of God is to be our authority. To make sure this is done, God gave the churches pastors and leaders in the church. They are to keep pure the teachings of the church. These heretics in Crete had no willingness to accept the authority of the Word of God or the apostolic authority within the church.

Paul described them as "foolish" talkers. Their speech doesn't make sense. It's empty talk. They claim to have the truth, but speak only nonsense. They speak clever words, but never produce the fruits of the Christian life. Their religious spiel sounds good, but their lives reveal their emptiness.

Their talk "blinds people to the truth." Literally, they are "mind deceivers." First they deceive themselves, and then others. Jesus called it the blind leading the blind. They are like a blind man in a dark room trying to tell someone how to find a black cat that is not there! We cannot let losers tell us how to win, and these heretics are losers. They have no victory, no happiness, yet try to tell us how to be happy and how to have victory.

They are "liars." The Apostle Paul quoted from one of the Cretan poets, Epimenides, who lived 600 years prior to the writing of this epistle. He said, "The Cretans are always liars." He based this upon the fact that the Cretans claimed that the tomb of the god Zeus was on their island. The Cretans chose *en masse* to believe and pass on this lie.

The word "liar" refers to deliberate deception. It very well may have been that the Cretans were proud of their bad influence and their bad reputation. They may have accepted the fact that Cretans were liars with pride. Likewise, heretics are deliberate liars and deceivers. They turn their heads away from the truth.

There were two aspects of this lying heresy. First, they

taught things they ought not to teach. They promoted false teachings. Second, their lying related to Jewish fables and commandments of men to turn away from the truth.

There has always been a magic intrigue about Jewish philosophies, ritual, and tradition. Consequently, in the early church there were many believers who insisted that one had to be circumcised in order to be a Christian. That was a carry-over from the old Jewish tradition and law. Gradually Jewish ritual and tradition became very significant in the early church in a way God did not intend. Some began to place great emphasis on eating certain kinds of foods and observing certain holy days. They stressed strict adherence to Jewish laws and traditions.

In Crete, they had begun to give great attention to Jewish fables and to commandments of men which took them away from God's truth. Man is basically proud. Give him a chance and he will make rules of his own, so he doesn't have to admit that he needs God. That is natural to all of us. One of the most difficult things about becoming a Christian is to recognize that we need God, that we have failed, that we cannot find happiness alone, that we stand guilty before God.

We see a similar situation in our own day. There are many rules or ideals that are passed off as being God's truth when they are simply ideas of men. For example, I have been in churches where people would be very upset if someone came in in a pantsuit. But in that same church, they would clap during a service. In other churches, this cannot be done. It's not "spiritual." But in those churches ladies wear pantsuits. The point I am making is that man has a tendency to take a particular, legalistic point of view and say, "This is what God wants." We take something like that and begin to build a system of doctrine or living upon it.

Wherever we are, God loves us. He has a journey he wants us to begin. The important thing for man to recognize is that he is a sinner who needs God and that God loves him and will save him if he will come in faith to him. If we are not careful, we will get hung up on religious fables and commandments of men that turn us away from God.

Paul was saying, "Place your major emphasis where God does." I am not for overthrowing traditions, but I know this: man-made traditions have no substantial significance to man's basic needs and God's basic provisions. Heretics are liars and deceivers. They have things backwards.

These men were like "lazy animals." The phrase means "rude, cruel, brutal." They were inconsiderate, arrogant people who lorded over others. Paul described them as "living only to satisfy their stomachs." The King James Version translates it "slow bellies." This interesting phrase doubtlessly referred to gluttons who had no self-control or self-restraint. The truth that we need to grasp is that man is to be mastered only by God and nothing else. He does not want us to have such an absence of self-restraint and self-control that we cannot walk with him in a disciplined life. The root meaning of these two words is "unemployed or lazy stomachs." He was saying that these heretics were less interested in working than they were in living off everybody else.

Let's stop and look at that from a physical standpoint. It says something very special for our day. We are building a society of unemployed people. Some don't want to be, many don't care. They can make more money being unemployed—let someone else pay their bills. This robs the individual of his initiative and pride, and destroys the very fabric of our society. Work is intended by God to be a dignity and a discipline. Work is to be an expression of our relationship with him. God thinks little of laziness.

Look at the spiritual aspect of this. The heretics wanted to be fed spiritually without investing themselves and their lives in the Word of God. They wanted to be blessed at the hand of God, but they wanted no responsibility. They wanted fellowship, as long as it didn't cost them anything. They wanted someone else to pay the bills, do the work, prepare the services. They had no intention of working for their spiritual food.

There is a similar feeling in our land today. We want to have the benefits of the church in our lives and communities. We want to have the blessings that come to God's people, but we don't want to help build that fellowship. We want to be fed without having any responsibilities. We want God's blessing without being in his service.

If that is our desire, we are holding a very subtle form of heresy. There is no spiritual food without spiritual commitment. A man must submit to God before the truth of the Word of God unfolds to him. He must surrender his heart, soul, and life if he is to receive spiritual blessings. That is true before a man is saved, and it continues to be true after salvation. Spiritual riches are not handouts thrown indiscriminately to Christian masses, but are given to loyal, obedient followers of Christ. God feeds us so we can feed others.

DEALING WITH THE HERETIC

"And it must be stopped. Already whole families have been turned away from the grace of God. Such teachers are only after your money. . . . And this is true. So speak to the Christians there as sternly as necessary to make them strong in the faith" (Titus 1:11, 13, TLB). This tells us three things about dealing with heretics.

First of all, they must be stopped (literally, "cut off"). They must be silenced; they must not be given liberty. How can we do this? By preaching the truth, by giving ourselves to the truth of the Word of God. When we do, we stop heresy and silence it.

The reason heretics must be stopped is that they capture whole families. Bear in mind that churches then did not have church buildings as we have. Most of the preaching was done from house to house. So we can see how it would be easy for the heretics to win families with their false teachings. God takes a very dim view of anything that destroys the fabric of the home. The home is God's institution, given to man before the church was given. It is the basic unit of Christian society. If the home is weak, the church dies and the gospel is made ineffective. Sabotage the family and the church is ineffective and unavailable to God's might and power.

It is very important for us to protect our homes. A Christian who spends all his time away from his family (even in God's service) is depriving them and the church of God's highest blessings. Our first responsibility after God is to the family, not the church.

We will never know peace in our homes until Jesus Christ is Lord of both husband and wife. God can make our homes to be a little bit of heaven, a foretaste of glory —but only if Jesus is in control. He has to be Lord.

Most of the unhappiness and distress in our families come from accepting a half-truth that deifies man and minimizes God. Guard your family from the heretics. They only want to fatten their own pocketbooks. They are looking out for themselves only.

We must also rebuke heretics. We are to let them know that they are wrong. In our day of tolerance and open-mindedness, we have become so broad-minded that we have become obscure, shallow, meaningless in what we say. In the letter of our Lord to Thyatira (Revelation 2), the only complaint God had was that they tolerated false teachings. We are to rebuke heresy sharply and take a firm stand against it.

Why should we rebuke heretics? So we can stand up and say, "I am smarter than you are, more intelligent than you are, more in touch with God than you are"? Do we do it so that we can put them down? No! Everything that we do is to be redemptive, "that they may be sound in the faith." Everything that we do is to lead people to Jesus Christ. We are to despise heresy, but love the heretic. We are to deal with them graciously. Although we may sharply rebuke what they say, we are to let them know that God loves them, so they may be whole in the faith.

We are to take that which is ill and make it well. We are to take that which is wrong and make it right. We are to take that which is unlovely and make it lovely. That is the purpose and intent of the church and the gospel. What a message of grace that is!

God meets us where we are. Wherever we are in our relationship with God, he longs to meet us there. Is there difficulty and stress? Is there rebellion? Is there unhappiness? God meets us there and will bring us to soundness and wholeness. That is the message of the gospel. That is why we are to keep our hearts committed to the Word of God, because as we do God will keep us in the mainstream, in touch with people. God will keep us caring. Together we will build healthy lives, healthy homes, healthy churches, and healthy communities. We need to combat heresy sternly but lovingly, to lead the heretics to a sound faith.

Conduct and
Character
*Titus 1:15, 16*

MEN HAVE ALWAYS FOUND it easy to think of themselves more highly than they should, to assume they are better than they really are. We too see very clearly the speck that is in someone else's eye, and not the beam that is in our own.

In Crete, there was great discussion concerning how a Christian ought to live and act, the relationship between what a person believes and what he does. In the first century, there was a subtle heresy called Gnosticism, a name based on the Greek word for "knowledge." It was a heresy which claimed superior spiritual knowledge to everyone else. Its adherents said, "We are God's elite. We have received special revelations from God, and because of this we want to give you some real insight into eternal truth."

One of the things they believed was that the body and the spirit were separate and could never be joined. What one believed in his heart had no bearing on what he did with his body. This gave license (and encouragement) for great misconduct. It allowed people to claim a belief in Jesus Christ and yet be immoral, dishonest, unkind, or ungodly. They believed that everything the body does is wrong, and everything the spirit does is right. In their minds, the two were totally separate.

This very subtle heresy expressed itself in various ways. The Jews on Crete laid great stress upon washing their hands and being ceremonially pure before they made the offering of the sacrifice. They were greatly concerned with proper ceremonial purity, but they were not so careful about personal purity. The Apostle Paul was declaring here that what a man believes in his heart is going to be demonstrated by how he lives with his body.

A DECLARATION

"Unto the pure all things are pure" (1:15). Some misunderstood that. Some thought that meant if one was pure in heart, he could do anything he wanted to. That is not what Paul was saying. A person who is pure is a person who seeks purity in all of life. A person who is pure has a life that matches what he says he believes.

It is important for us to understand that Paul was not talking about personal purity that we can acquire through personal discipline, a purity of doing our best and eliminating our bad habits. The Bible clearly states none is righteous, none of us is pure. Our righteousness, our own purity is like filthy rags in the sight of God (Isaiah 64:6). Paul is not talking about an acquired purity, but a bestowed purity, something only God can produce. This comes when the grace of God touches a man's life.

Then we are judged righteous, accounted pure because God has given his purity to us.

The New Testament principle is this: He who knew no sin became sin for us, so that we who had no righteousness might become righteous in him (2 Corinthians 5:21). It is his righteousness in us, his purity we are talking about. All who are truly pure have come to Jesus Christ. They have confessed their sins and have received forgiveness and righteousness that only God can give.

Now, to a person who has experienced this kind of purity, all things are pure. Everything that he seeks in life is pure. Purity of conduct characterizes the life of such a person. Paul told the Corinthian church that if any man is in Christ, he is a new creature; old things have passed away, all has become new (2 Corinthians 5:17). There is a change in character, a change in heart. The believer seeks purity. Whenever his life does not measure up to what God requires of him, the Spirit of God within him brings him to repentance and cleansing. He moves along the way of purity.

Many people accuse Christianity of being a negative religion, dealing only with prohibitions. Paul's declaration here was a positive statement. When a man receives righteousness and purity from God, he is changed. He has a new heart and a new life. This does not mean that he won't sin again, but when he does the Spirit of God convicts him. He will not rest easy when he is disobedient to God. He is a person whose life is directed toward purity.

When we say we belong to Christ, we ought to live

like it. A Christian should practice what he preaches. A Christian should demonstrate in all he does that he belongs to Jesus Christ. There is so much of the world in the lives of the people in the church that it has neutralized the power and progress of the church. This ought not to be. God's people should be tuned in to the Spirit of God. Purity must be the hallmark of the Christian. That is the plain declaration of the Word of God. The idea that one can belong to God and live like the devil is heresy. Those who know Christ hunger to be like him. The great hope of the Christian life is to see him and to be like him.

## A DEFILEMENT

"Unto the pure all things are pure, but unto them that are defiled and unbelieving is nothing pure; but even their mind and conscience is defiled" (1:15). It is interesting that the Christian is described with one word, "pure," while the lost person is described with two words, "defiled and unbelieving." The word "defiled" means "to stain something another color, to dye." Thus, the object is marked and stained. It means to pollute, to rot, to cheapen in such a way that it cannot be changed.

That is what sin does to us. Sin marks us. Sin stains our lives. Sin corrupts our hearts and souls. Sin destroys everything that it touches, except as the power of God and the touch of the Holy Spirit in our lives defeat it.

How does a person's life get to be stained? Look at the word "unbelieving." It literally means "without faith." The problem they had in the churches in Crete is the same problem we face today—the lack of faith in God and his purposes. Many people say, "I believe Jesus came into the world. I am confident that he lived, died on the cross, and was raised from the dead." Intellectually they believe, but they do not trust him personally. People are corrupted when they have an intellectual knowledge only.

Just knowing about God and Jesus Christ is not sufficient to be saved. A man is not saved because he accepts facts about Jesus, but because he trusts in Jesus. There are many people who have a head knowledge of Christ, but do not have a heart knowledge of Christ. Those who have been defiled are people without faith. I can think of no greater tragedy than for a person to know all about God and not know God.

On our trip through the Middle East some years ago, our Arab guide knew more about Jesus Christ than I did. He knew everything Jesus had done. He repeated the teachings of Jesus Christ. Yet when I approached him and asked him if he had ever given his heart to Christ he said, "I am a Moslem by birth, and I cannot do that." He knew all about Jesus Christ but did not know him. I wonder if we do not have people like that in our churches. They know about Christ, but they are without faith. The result is that their minds and consciences are defiled.

We cannot imagine anything worse than that. Here is a man whose thoughts turn only toward evil. He sees only vulgar, repulsive things. His mind contains only garbage. His conscience is so seared that nothing is wrong, nothing seems to convict him. He feels no guilt. There is no awareness of need. That is what happens when a man lives without faith.

If we do not have that inward relationship with Jesus Christ, that is the inevitable result. Jesus talked about religious people who had no personal faith. "Yes, woe upon you, Pharisees, and you other religious leaders—hypocrites! For you tithe down to the last mint leaf in your garden, but ignore the important things—justice and mercy and faith. Yes, you should tithe, but you shouldn't leave the more important things undone. Blind guides! You strain out a gnat and swallow a camel. . . . You are so careful to polish the outside of the cup, but the inside is foul with extortion and greed. . . . First cleanse the inside of the cup, and then the whole cup will be clean" (Matthew 23:23-26, TLB). They looked good on the outside, but inside there was nothing but rotten-ness, corruption, sickness, and death. The inside must be clean before the outside can be right.

It does not matter how good and proper we may be in the eyes of men. It matters not how much outward honesty and integrity we may have if things are not right inside. Without faith, our minds and consciences are distorted. The conscience can be trained. Many times in our society we have seen people commit crimes without any apparent remorse or guilt. That is what happens when we have no faith in Jesus Christ. When we live a life of reliance upon ourselves, relying upon what we can do, upon our own character and righteousness, we will inevitably come to a place of corruption and defilement. We will not have minds that are sensitive to that which is right.

A DECEPTION

It is bad enough to be defiled, but it is worse to try to deceive people about it. "They profess that they know God; but in works they deny him, being abominable, and disobedient, and unto every good word reprobate" (1:16). A claimed knowledge of God without holy living is hypocritical. "He that saith, I know him, and keepeth not his commandments, is a liar, and the truth is not in him" (1 John 2:4). "If a man say, I love God, and hateth his brother, he is a liar" (1 John 4:20). Jesus said, "If ye love me, keep my commandments" (John 14:15). If our hearts are right, we will live a life that is turned toward God.

This does not mean sinless perfection. It does mean that our lives are in tune with God, and when we sin our hearts condemn us. We move forward in the path of purity that God has for us. People who say one thing and live another are practicing deception.

God declares three things about such deception. First, it is "abominable." That word literally means "detestable." God declares that he is disgusted with such a thing. We cannot find any English expression of disgust that would be stronger than this word. God declared the same thing to the prophet Isaiah: "I am sick of your sacrifices. Don't bring me any more of them. I don't want your fat rams; I don't want to see the blood from your offerings. Who wants your sacrifices when you have no sorrow for your sins? The incense you bring me is a stench in my nostrils. Your holy celebrations of the new moon and the Sabbath, and your special days for fasting —even your most pious meetings—all are frauds! I want nothing more to do with them" (Isaiah 1:11-13, TLB).

They are also "disobedient." This is a characteristic that we would expect of these people. The word "disobedient" literally refers to a person who refuses to obey although he is admonished and urged to be obedient. He knows, he has heard, but he makes a deliberate choice to rebel. If one has a life that is corrupt and stained, if one is a person without faith, it's not surprising that he spurns all urging to do right.

Paul further called such a person "reprobate." The best equivalent we have is "worthless." This person is worthless as far as good works are concerned. The literal translation would be "rejected after testing." Everybody who makes a profession is going to be tested as to whether he really meant what he said, whether he was really willing to do what God said. In this case, the people have been tested and have been rejected. They have been found to be liars.

This is not to say that a person who is not a Christian does not do some "good" things. That is not the point. Paul is saying that all the good things that a non-Christian may do are worthless as far as relationship with God is concerned. They have no eternal value. A person who is not a Christian may go on a campaign to feed the hungry. That is a good thing. But if all we do is give people something for the hour and not something to guide them through life and eternity, we are failures. A person who is rebellious toward God only gives others surface things that are ultimately worthless in the sight of God. Even the good works of the nonbeliever are reprobate.

The appeal to our hearts is very simple. It is for us to

live what we say we believe. If we have given our hearts to Christ, we ought to live like it. There must be a difference in our lives after we are saved. The greatest tragedy in the world is people who say they are Christians and live for Satan. They talk like the world, act like the world, have the habits of the world, and do the same things as the world. There are many people who say they belong to Christ, but do not live in a way that honors him. That brings God sadness.

# 5

The Fruit
of Sound
Doctrine
*Titus 2:1-3*

SOUND DOCTRINE is at the heart of the New Testament church. We need to believe the right things, to hold the right doctrinal positions. We need to allow the Holy Spirit to give us a glimpse of the truth and then stand upon that truth. "But speak thou the things which become sound doctrine" (2:1). As we do this, we will then be able to implement in our churches all that the Apostle Paul was encouraging Titus to do in the churches of Crete.

Doctrine is not popular today. Many ask, "Does it really matter what we believe?" Some say that God is in all men, all men are brothers, we are all moving toward the same goal by different roads—so whatever we believe, we're OK. This is a very subtle form of heresy that takes away the urgency of the gospel.

We cannot have healthy churches without healthy doctrine. To get things in focus, we need to go back to the first chapter. There the great apostle says of false teachers, "They profess that they know God; but in their works they deny him, being abominable, and disobedient, and unto every good work reprobate" (1:16).

THE CONTRAST

In 1:16 Paul says "they" and in 2:1 he says "thou." They are this way, but you are not to be like that. They are hypocrites—they profess to know God, yet live like the devil—their lives and beliefs are opposites. That is the way *they* are, but you should not be so. You must be consistent in what you say and in what you do. Here is a strong appeal for godly behavior, for wholeness of life.

If we want to defeat heresy, we shouldn't spend all our time trying to discredit the heretics or the things they say. To discredit heresy, we need simply to preach the truth and stand firmly on the Word of God. We must live a life before the world that declares that what we preach is truth.

Sometimes we give too much publicity and recognition to the heretic. We really combat heresy by preaching the truth, living the truth, and standing on the truth.

This puts a big burden on us to teach the right things. We must make sure we base our lives upon the Word of God. If we want to know how our relationships should be—husband to wife, parent to child, employee to employer, friend to friend—then we should look in the Word of God. As we make our lives consistent with the Word, we combat heresy.

"Speak thou the things which become sound doctrine" (2:1). The word "become" literally means "to become conspicuously fit." It refers to something that is very obviously healthy and wholesome. Sound doctrine is healthy truth. What we preach ought to make people well. What we proclaim ought to encourage people. It should be appropriate for a saving gospel. We have a gospel of forgiveness, so we ought to demonstrate forgiveness. We have a gospel of love, so we ought to show love. We should speak the things that bring health and wholeness to people's lives.

THE CONCEPT

The great apostle now turns from the preacher to the layman. It is imperative for a church to have godly ministers, but the church must also have godly members. A Christlike preacher is important, but a Christlike congregation is just as essential. If we are going to reach the world with the gospel, it will never be done simply by preaching from the pulpit. No great church is built solely on preaching.

All Christians are to be the pattern for the church. The burden is upon every Christian, not only the preacher. There was no double standard in the New Testament, one for the minister and another for the one who sat under his ministry. In the New Testament church, they were all together in the service of God.

Paul gave Titus instructions for the entire church. He began with the older people: "Teach the older men to be serious and unruffled; they must be sensible, knowing and believing the truth and doing everything with love and patience" (2:2, TLB). Paul was not talking about spiritual age, but physical, men with many years behind them.

The older men are to be godly men. I used to think that when one got old, he would automatically be a nice old man. That is not true. There are a lot of grouchy old men! If we are going to be gentle and gracious in old age, we must have some practice. We will not get that way automatically when we get to be sixty-five. Godly, kind older people are that way because they began when they were younger.

The older men are to be "sober" ("temperate" in most versions). They must not be abusive in their uses of alcohol. In the ancient world, wine was used for various purposes. But that which was meant to be medicinal and helpful should not be used in a way to bring harm.

The older men should be "grave" or "serious." That doesn't mean they can't smile, or that they should be long-faced all the time. Rather, they are to realize they have a very serious task in life. They have traveled a long way down the road of life, and younger believers are now patterning themselves after them. Older men must be completely serious about being what God wants them to be; for if they fall, some other Christians will stumble too.

Older men are to be serious about the Word of God. Older men ought to be gifted in sharing the Word of God. It is one of their responsibilities to have a grasp of it.

The apostle used the word "temperate" (KJV) also. That refers to one who has self-control, who has given himself to God in such a way that he is not overindulgent. He is in control of his life because he has committed it to God.

He has learned how to bring his body under subjection. The Apostle Paul elsewhere stated that he constantly struggled with his human flesh to bring it under control, so it would not dominate him (1 Corinthians 9:27). Older men have their lives anchored in the Holy Spirit, and so are protected against excesses.

They should also be "sound in faith." I don't know why the definite article does not appear in the English, but it did in the Greek. This verse literally means that they ought to be healthy "in *the* faith." The older men must know what they believe. They must stand upon the Word of God.

They are also to exhibit "love." Again, the definite article was there and literally means "in *the* love." "The love" is *agape* in the Greek, which you recognize as being used frequently in the New Testament. This word describes the love of God, a God-kind of love.

In addition, older men are to be "sound in patience." One of the things Jesus commended in the church at Thyatira was patience (Revelation 2:19). The same Greek word is used here. It literally means "peace under pressure," peace of heart despite pressure of mind and body. This is total and complete confidence in God regardless of the circumstances.

In the midst of turmoil, in the midst of difficulty, in the midst of disappointment, in the midst of heartache, one can anchor his life to God; his heart can enjoy peace. The older men ought to be like that. They should be the kind of people who, when pressures rise and circumstances are strained, have a sense of peace because God is in control.

Paul declared that the older women ought to be "in behavior as becometh holiness, not false accusers, not given to much wine, teachers of good things" (2:3). There is nothing quite as beautiful and attractive as a godly woman. There is a quality of life that God can give to a woman who walks with him that is something very special. The reverse is also true. Satan uses nothing quite so easily as a promiscuous woman.

Paul is not referring to their being "teachers of good things" in the church, but about their teaching in the home, day by day, in their overall example. This is much broader than simply standing to teach a Bible class. It is the teaching that takes place by the example and the life day by day, in and out of the home.

They are to be "in behavior as becometh holiness." The word "behavior" literally means "demeanor" and refers to the disposition of the mind, a way of thinking. Here is someone whose character is sacred, whose life is characterized by wholeness and holiness. When we are around her, we know she walks with the Lord. She is clearly no stranger to holy things.

The phrase "false accusers" is the translation of the Greek word *diabolos*, also used for the devil. The New Testament tells us that Satan accuses the saints before the throne of God (Revelation 12:10). The older women must not be guilty of slander or malicious gossip. That does not befit a holy and godly person. They should rather be speaking words that lift up, healthy, wholesome words. That is good advice for all of us.

Further, they should not be "given to much wine." The Greek word *doulos* is the word used here and is usually translated "slaves." The women should not be slaves to wine. The Word of God recognizes that there are some legitimate uses of alcohol. Many of our medicines and drugs have alcoholic content. But the Bible also recognizes the dangers of abusing alcohol. That is the warning here.

Older women are to be "teachers of good things." This refers to the good things of God, the good things of life, things too great and too significant for us to miss by going after unimportant things. Women teach by their lives, by their words, by all that they are.

The Bible gives great deference to senior citizens in the church. Nothing quite blesses a church like godly older people who through their years have given themselves to God. They often demonstrate beautiful self-control, a sweet humility of spirit, and a deep, genuine love that the Holy Spirit has produced. They exemplify a wholesome, sound faith and knowledge of the truth. Many older people lead the church in such a godly spirit.

We should thank God for those who have gone before us. We are, today, the product of our past. We stand not as individuals who start on nothing, but we stand based upon the lives of those who have gone before us—our parents, our grandparents. We owe much to those who went before. As members of the church of Jesus Christ, we should honor and thank God for those older people whom God has given us. They are a special blessing to our hearts.

The other side of this is that the elderly should pray to God that he will make them gracious and kind in old age, that God will allow his wisdom to rest in them so that they can reflect Christ to the younger ones. The years rob us of strength. We can no longer climb mountains as easily as when we were young. But we can help others by letting God use our lives. As older persons, we should pray that God will help us to be an encouragement in the church and the community. We are not on the shelf.

Throughout all of life, there is the capacity for growth. Each of us, regardless of our age, should commit ourselves to God now, so that as the years pass we will be able to be what God needs us to be then. That challenge is for every one of us.

This may mean some changes for us now. It may mean that we need to commit our lives to God in a way that we have never done before. If we are going to be what God wants us to be in old age, we must be what God wants us to be now.

None of us likes to think about growing old. Time gets away from us. The devil steals from us. This is why the New Testament declares that the Holy Spirit yearns over us with a godly jealousy (James 4:5). That means that the Holy Spirit is jealous of every moment that Satan steals from us. If Satan can steal one minute from us, he can steal two. If he can get two, he can get sixty. If he can get a week, then a month or a year. Before we know it, time has gone by and the things that we should have done have slipped by.

Now is God's time. We must start now if we are to become the godly older people God wants us to be.

# Good Advice to Young Adults
## *Titus 2:4-8*

FOLLOWING THE ADVICE to older Christians, we find instructions to young adults. "That they may teach the young women to be sober, to love their husbands, to love their children, to be discreet, chaste, keepers at home, good, obedient to their own husbands, that the Word of God be not blasphemed. Young men likewise exhort to be sober-minded. In all things showing thyself a pattern of good works: in doctrine showing uncorruptness, gravity, sincerity, sound speech, that cannot be condemned; that he that is of the contrary part may be ashamed, having no evil thing to say of you" (2:4-8).

AN EXHORTATION
The word "exhort" (verse 6) is very important to our understanding. *The Living Bible* translates it "urge." It means "to plead, to lovingly urge, to tenderly and compassionately give counsel and advice." This is the very opposite of a domineering, high-handed, demanding type of appeal. This tender term characterizes how we

should minister the Word of God—we must serve with love, tenderness, and kindness.

In guiding and counseling those who are younger than we, we must use tenderness and love, a gracious urging.

The young women were exhorted to be "sober," the same word we saw in 1:8, meaning to have self-control in your thought life, to know what you believe and why, and to be serious about it.

The next two phrases may seem obvious. Why would a young mother have to be admonished to love her husband and her children? We need to grasp the historical setting to understand this. Before Jesus Christ came, women were simply considered pieces of property. They had no real place in society. They had no status, but were considered slaves bound to their husbands. Jesus' gospel lifted women up and put them in partnership with their husbands. The gospel linked their lives together. In marriage, two become one flesh so that they move as one, breathe as one, live as one. That is God's ideal.

In Crete, some Christian women were taking advantage of their newfound freedom. They began to put themselves above their husbands and to neglect their particular responsibilities, even to the point of being unfaithful. Thus, they were admonished to love their husbands.

They were also to love their children. In Crete, the women had given themselves to pleasure and activities outside the home. They had no particular interest in their children, so they were reminded to love their children. This is a call for unselfish love, genuine love that sacrifices itself for those children.

Our society needs this exhortation. Many wives work, usually out of necessity. But whatever else they might do, they must give themselves sacrificially, lovingly, genuinely to their children.

They were also told to be "discreet," the same Greek word that we found in verse 2 where it is translated "temperate." It simply means "self-control." It means we should not be dominated by anything or anyone except God. We must not become slaves to habit. We must not be undisciplined in our personal lives. We need to obey the will of God in our lives.

They were further to be taught to be "chaste" or "pure." We cannot read very much of Titus without being aware that God calls for a genuine morality on the part of the Christian. Our lives ought to parallel whatever we say we believe. We must not say we love God if our lives do not honor him. We are to live pure lives. This admonition applies to both the unmarried and the married. For those unmarried, it is a command to keep oneself for marriage, to keep pure and chaste, open to the touch of God. Many young women in Crete were unfaithful to their husbands and saw nothing wrong with their immorality and promiscuity. It was acceptable in their society. Paul told Titus to instruct them to be pure.

There needs to be an old-fashioned revival of purity among God's people, so the Word of God will not be ridiculed. When we do not live our profession, God is mocked. We must be pure.

"Keepers at home" literally means "domesticated." That implies that the wife should stay home, that the woman's place is to build the home. She does this in partnership with her husband. Because of his responsibilities outside the home, she has a unique responsibility in it. The home is her top priority.

The word "good" simply means to be kind and gracious. Young women should be kind to their families and to those in the fellowship of the church. They should have a gracious attitude toward others.

"Obedient to their own husbands" does not mean blind servitude. Because of the tendency of these young women to disassociate themselves from their husbands, Paul is declaring that they are bound inseparably to them. A wife has been joined by God to her husband. Thus, she is to cling to him, submit to him, and walk in harmony with him. There must be a unity and oneness demonstrated by an obedient life together in the Lord.

The reason for all of this exhortation is "that the word of God be not blasphemed." If young women failed in their homes, then a pagan society would laugh at the Word of God. People would say, "What kind of gospel is that? You say it brings life, but look at your lives and your homes. They are no different from ours." Again, our faith must affect every part of our lives.

The greatest threat from within Christianity today is hypocrisy. The person who says, "I am a Christian, I belong to Christ," yet has an empty and shallow life, is an affront to the cause of Christ. If the young women do not live as instructed, the Word of God will be blasphemed.

Then there was an exhortation to the young men: "Young men likewise exhort to be sober-minded." It is interesting that this was all he told the young men. The young women had nine things to do, the young men only one! The word "sober-minded" commanded him to be serious about his responsibilities.

But upon close examination we find that God put greater responsibility upon the man than the woman. The woman is to submit herself to her husband as unto the Lord (Ephesians 5:22). But the man is to love his wife as Christ loved the church (Ephesians 5:25). The man has a responsibility under God to love his wife with the same intensity, with the same deep and sacrificing love that Jesus demonstrated when he gave himself for the church.

Some of us husbands worry because our wives do not submit to us. If we loved them like Jesus loved the church, it would make a difference. If we take seriously the admonition of Christ, if we are sober-minded, we will become the spiritual spearhead in the home. We have the responsibility to be godly men in our homes. That is our assignment from God.

AN EXAMPLE
"In all things showing thyself a pattern of good works" (2:7). The word "pattern" describes an impression made upon an object by the pounding of a hammer upon a seal. It means "an exact reproduction." In this context, it could very well mean "an example of good works."

We ought to be so much in tune with God that when

people see and hear us, they will know that what we are saying is what we are living and that what we are living is worthy of reproduction. That is a big task for the church.

Now we are told how to do this. "In doctrine showing uncorruptness, gravity, sincerity" (2:7). Our doctrine is to be pure or correct, sincerely held with serious devotion, solidly based on the Word of God. "Sound speech" (2:8) means "wholesome and healthy speech." When such a person speaks, we know he is telling the pure truth. If we listen to what he says, it will bring happiness to our lives and meaning to our homes.

"That he that is of the contrary part may be ashamed." If anyone criticizes what we say, he should be embarrassed because it is obvious that we have said the right thing. He will have nothing to say to us to condemn us.

We should speak words of counsel and witness that are healthy and life-giving. While we debate the gifts of the Spirit, eschatological chronologies, and various other items of theology, people are dying in sin all around us. Satan is rubbing his hands together in glee while we are preoccupied with lesser things.

There is nothing good about bad doctrine. But it is equally bad for us to say the right thing in the wrong way. Let's be sure we don't speak the truth in anger or bitterness, but in love and concern. Let's not say the right things with the wrong spirit.

The only way we can speak the truth in love is to be sure that today and every day we have bowed our hearts to Christ. There will come a day when Christ will estab-

lish his kingdom on the earth, and all the victory pur-
chased at Calvary will be seen and heard by all! Until
then, our responsibility is to be faithful, to be true to the
commitment that we have made to Christ.

Facing
Responsibility
*Titus 2:9, 10*

"EXHORT SERVANTS to be obedient unto their own masters, and to please them well in all things; not answering again; not purloining, but showing all good fidelity; that they may adorn the doctrine of God our Saviour in all things" (2:9, 10). The word "servants" means "slaves." On the surface that appears to apply only to people who lived in an age of slavery. What could it possibly say to me in a land of freedom and democracy, a land where the shackles have been removed?

The Apostle Paul was not endorsing slavery in these verses. Christianity was never intended to change society, but to change people. When people change, society changes.

Paul was not urging us to support the status quo and not rock the boat. He was not telling us to accept society as we find it. Rather, he was telling slaves to be the best slaves possible, because that was the only way they would win their masters to Christ, the only way they could faithfully spread the gospel.

He was encouraging believing slaves to not feel downhearted or cheated, but to be the very best slaves possible and so get the very most out of their slavery. Rather than condoning slavery, Paul was sowing the seeds to destroy slavery. If we follow the gospel to its ultimate conclusion, slavery would be impossible.

The Bible doesn't give us counsel only if we have a certain set of circumstances. Rather, the Word of God teaches us how to behave and think in every situation. It applies to all of us, slave or free. Whatever our circumstances may be, God has a word for us.

The principles in this passage are helpful not only to slaves, but to all of us who have the responsibility of being God's children in the world.

THE ASSIGNMENT GIVEN

It was God's will "to be obedient unto their own masters." The word "obedient" was used to describe a company of soldiers as they stand at attention and salute their commander. They are declaring as they stand at attention in front of him that they are ready to take his orders.

These slaves were to follow completely the orders of their masters. The word "master" is the Greek word from which we get our word "despot." They were to be in subjection to the commands of the despot, the dictator who owned them. They were not to start a revolution and endeavor to change things. The way to change their circumstances was to be the kind of slaves they should be, and this included obeying their masters.

They were further "to please them well in all things." The slave was to do everything he was told to do, unless it contradicted what God had told him to do. For example, if their masters (or our employers) told them to be immoral, then they would be compelled to refuse, since God forbids immorality.

Paul further admonished that they were not to talk back. "Not answering again" literally means "not to talk back or argue with someone." We must not say, "That isn't fair. You shouldn't ask me to do that." We shouldn't thwart our master's plans or try to defeat his purpose.

"Not purloining" means "not taking what belongs to another." Slaves were not to steal from their masters. This has real application in our day. I try to be very meticulous about this. When I write personal letters that are not related to the church work, I pay for those letters. I do not feel it is the church's place to pay for my personal correspondence. It is very important that we do not purloin, that we do not take what belongs to our masters or employers. On-the-job theft is a tremendous problem in our society. As Christians, we should be free of this.

"Showing all good fidelity" simply means that the slave was to be faithful. That was hard for the slave to do. Their masters did not always appreciate them or take good care of them. It was difficult for a slave to be faithful to a man who mistreated him.

The principles involved here apply to us in our relationship to our employers. Whatever we are instructed to do, we ought to do it unless it is a violation of conscience. We are to please our employers and supervisors in all things, not talk back, not argue with them, not contradict them. If we are in a position where we can express our opinions, that's fine; but do not try to thwart their plans. Do not take what does not belong to you. Always be faithful. These are God's ideals.

## AN ASSESSMENT MADE

If we perform the assignment God has given us to do, the resulting assessment will be: "That they may adorn the doctrine of God our Saviour in all things." Paul didn't use the word "adorn" with husband, wife, or children, but only with slaves. It is an unusual word in the New Testament, coming from the Greek word *kosmos*. We speak about the cosmic organization of the world, the orderly nature of the universe. *Kosmos* refers to a system where there is order, where we can anticipate what is going to happen, where there is a sense of organization, purpose, and direction.

"Adorn" is the verb from that word. It literally means to take precious jewels and arrange them so as to show their true beauty.

If these slaves would do the assignment that was given to them, they would display the doctrines of God in such a way that they would be a blessing to the whole world. They had an opportunity to do something that no one else could do. They were suffering under the hand of oppression; but if they would take it in the spirit of godliness and love, they would display the beauty of the truth of God in a way that would win those who reviewed it.

Paul is speaking to oppressed people of all ages. Whenever people find themselves in unjust circumstances, they are to demonstrate the grace of God and the love of Christ. By so living, they display the truth of God in such a way that people will want to possess it.

What Paul was saying throughout the entire book of Titus is that if we really belong to God, our lives will show it. People will be able to see it. They will look at our lives and notice something that is appealing and attractive. Thus we will adorn the doctrine of God, we will display it and so arrange it that people will say "Wow! Beautiful! What a wonderful thing!"

But we are to go beyond "adorning" and "adorn the doctrine of God our Saviour *in all things*." The phrase "in all things" is neuter and could be translated "among all people." Now we begin to see what Paul was talking about. If slaves would be the kind of Christians that he challenged them to be, they would permeate all of society. They would adorn the doctrine of God among all people. People may not be surprised if a well-to-do man stands and says, "I have given my life to God and he is in my heart." Someone may observe, "Well, if I had what he has, I could do that too." But whoever demonstrates loyalty to God from a position of oppression and servitude will be a marvel for all people. There must be something to what such a person says.

I want to make two concluding observations from this passage. First, real freedom is not dependent on circumstances. Some of the freest people I have seen have been in jail. God liberated them while they were behind bars. Jesus said, "Ye shall know the truth, and the truth shall make you free" (John 8:32). He was speaking to Jews being ruled by the Roman Empire. They were oppressed but free.

When Jesus Christ comes into our lives, we have a spiritual freedom that does not depend on our circumstances. Whether we have much or little, we are liberated, happy, content.

Do we have circumstances we do not desire? We are out of work? We have difficult trials? God can change those circumstances; but even more important, he can change us in the midst of them and make us free.

There is a second application. If a slave on the island of Crete was instructed to be faithful to his earthly master, how much more should I, a slave of Christ, be faithful to my Master! Over and over again the Apostle Paul said, "I am a slave, a servant of Jesus Christ." That is the same word used here. When a person is saved, he is a slave to Jesus Christ; yet he has never been more free.

As a servant and slave, I am to be obedient to my Master. Whatever God says, I am to do. I am to be perfectly content as his servant. I am standing before him as a soldier, ready to respond. I am his to command. I am to please my Lord in all things, in every way, at all times. He is my Lord. I will not contradict him. I will not answer back again. Do I find myself in circumstances that test my faith? He is the master, I am the slave. He is under no obligation to do anything for me that does not please him. But whatever pleases him is best for me. I must simply obey.

I must not steal from him. What an application that is

for us Christians. I must not take what belongs to him. For example, the church is his, not mine. I must be careful about giving credit to someone else that really belongs to God. I must keep good faith in all things.

If I keep faithfully what God has committed to me, I will adorn the doctrine of God; I will display it for all the world to see and they will desire it. They will be attracted to it. They will love our Lord and commit their lives to him. It will spread like wildfire.

When we determine we are slaves of God, of Jesus Christ, and give ourselves as such to him, people all over the earth will be drawn to him.

# Grace for This World
## Titus 2:11, 12

NOW THE APOSTLE PAUL turned to the subject of the grace of God, which is sufficient for any circumstance (even slavery, as we have already seen).

"For the grace of God that bringeth salvation hath appeared to all men, teaching us that, denying ungodliness and worldly lusts, we should live soberly, righteously, and godly, in this present world" (2:11, 12).

## THE PURPOSE OF GRACE

"Grace" is a term we often toss around very flippantly. What is grace? What is its purpose?

God's grace is something desperately needed but not deserved, something that one might receive but has no right to expect. We are not just talking about human grace, but the grace of God—God acting toward us in a way that we do not expect and do not deserve.

There is daily evidence that man is a sinner. In the most enlightened and most affluent age that has ever dawned upon the earth, we have the highest divorce rate, the highest suicide rate, the highest crime rate, the highest war rate ever to be found among men. We are not good, not any of us.

We would expect God to respond in anger, judgment, and punishment. Instead, he offers us grace. We deserve wrath, but God says, "I will give you forgiveness. I cannot let your sin go unpunished, so I will take the punishment for you. I will sacrifice myself in your behalf." That is the purpose of his grace. He wants to forgive us.

Further, it is the grace of God "that bringeth salvation." The phrase "bringeth salvation" is an adjective. Paul was literally saying, "the salvation-bringing grace of God has appeared!" The ultimate purpose of God's grace is that we might receive forgiveness, that we might enter the family of God. Every time God has spared our lives, every time God has given us wisdom for decisions, every time God has moved in miraculous ways in our lives, it was for the purpose of bringing us to salvation and then to maturity in Christ.

THE PRESENCE OF GRACE

This grace "hath appeared to all men," a phrase meaning "to be made evident." It refers to something that was once hidden, but now is brought to light. God has unveiled it.

How did God do this? Did he show his grace by sending us the Bible? That was a precious thing to do, but that is not the primary evidence of God's grace. Did we learn of his grace through a beautiful song? No, it was revealed by Jesus. Paul is underscoring the importance and centrality of the incarnation of Jesus Christ. Grace has become visible in the person of Jesus Christ.

Some believe that all men will be saved because of Jesus Christ. That is certainly what God wants. God does not desire that any should perish, but wants all to come to repentance (2 Peter 3:9). But what God is saying here is that this salvation-bringing grace has become apparent so that all may have access to it. The advent of Christ did not mean that all men everywhere would be saved, but that all men could be saved. Every man has the opportunity to respond to the claims of Christ for his life.

That's why we gather as a church week by week. We do not gather simply to pat ourselves on the back and think about how spiritual we are, or even about how nice God is being to us. We have banded together as a church because Christ is the visible evidence of the salvation-bringing grace of God. It is our assignment to see that men everywhere hear the message of our God who loves them.

THE PRODUCT OF GRACE

Verse 12 begins with a reminder that we are to be taught through the appearance of this grace revealed by Jesus Christ. Many people have the idea that Christianity is just one grand experience after another, one gigantic high, one great mountaintop experience. Knowing Jesus is a wonderful experience, but what is revealed here is that there is a direction that God's grace will take in our lives. It will express itself as we are taught. The grace of God is a teaching grace.

There is more to God's plan for your life than being saved. God is just beginning a wonderful experience of maturity. He is moving us on toward growth. He is teaching and instructing us.

Much of the unhappiness among professing Christians is because of a half-hearted, undisciplined approach to the Christian faith. We need to be instructed in genuine Christian commitment. That is the product of grace, teaching us that there is more. We have not arrived. Paul mentioned two negatives and three positives in this connection.

We are to "deny ungodliness." This means to turn away from, to reject, to turn loose of "ungodliness" (literally, "without godliness"). We are to deny anything that is not in keeping with the Spirit of God, whose we are and in whom we live and abide and have our very being.

Next, we are admonished to deny "worldly lusts." "Worldly" is the Greek word *kosmos*. In our English language we use this word to describe the world system. Coupled with the word "lusts," which refers to strong, passionate desires, it represents the idea of involving ourselves in the system of evil that is presently operating in the world. We cannot draw our sustenance from the world.

We too often allow the world to set our standards for us. We allow the world to make decisions for us. Even in the church we may have worldly ideas and goals if we are not very careful. We are not to let this world system of evil, which is under the control and power of Satan, to be a companion in our hearts and lives. We are to reject it and draw away from it.

We are instructed now to "live soberly." We have encountered that word several times in Titus. It literally means "self-control." Jesus Christ lives in us and wants to be Lord in our lives. We are to be spiritually controlled because we have bowed before Christ. Thus, we are to live as though Christ were living his life through us (which he is!). We are to live a life of self-control, a disciplined life, bowing before Christ as our Lord. If our life is in control, under the leadership of the Spirit of God, we will have no trouble rejecting ungodliness and worldly lusts.

Further, we are to "live righteously." The word "righteously" is a word that refers to how we conduct ourselves toward our fellowmen. We must live in such a way that we do not take advantage of, are not unkind to, not critical of, do not bear hatred toward those around us.

Many times we let others determine what kind of people we are going to be. If they are angry toward us, we are angry toward them. We are told here to live in such a way that this will not be true. In our contacts with those around us, we must let God's life in us make our relationships sweet and happy. Do not harbor anger, bitterness, and the things that are normal to the natural man. Live in a way that is above and beyond that. Live righteously.

Now we are instructed to "live godly." That simply means to live like God. It means that our responses and reactions should be like his responses and reactions. You may say, "You don't understand my temper, you don't understand my kids, you just don't know my parents, you don't have to live with this husband I have, you don't know what kind of wife I have, what an employer, what a situation... you don't understand!"

If we are to live like God in all of those constant relationships, we must know God. To know God, we must have a daily walk with him. There is no such thing as instant godliness. It is hard work. We must discipline ourselves to spend time with God, time in his Word, time in worship. That is how God is going to be able ultimately to see that our responses are like his.

"Let this mind be in you, which was also in Christ Jesus" (Philippians 2:5). How do we do that? By spending time with God so that our reactions are like his. That is the product of God's grace.

Now Paul reached a significant conclusion. The salvation-bringing grace of God has become visible for all men in the person of Jesus Christ. As that grace gets into our lives, it instructs us that we need to turn our backs on ungodliness and worldly lusts, live righteously, soberly, and godly right now *"in this present world"*! In this world, in all circumstances, we must do as God instructs us. Even under adverse conditions (including "slavery"), we can do it in this present day. Let none of us say to God, "I can't do it. My job is too hard. You don't understand the situation that I'm in. I cannot live like that." In ourselves we cannot do it. But if we have received God's salvation-bringing grace, that grace will produce that kind of life.

Whatever our circumstances, God is able to bring victory into our lives. We need a faith that can look into each new day and say, "This is the day which the Lord hath made; we will rejoice and be glad in it" (Psalm 118:24). Where do we get such a faith? From the Lord. He wants to be that kind of strength in us. But this will be our experience only if we turn from our worldly pursuits and surrender to the Lord in a fresh way so that we can live in the present world like God.

Christ's
Glorious
Appearing
*Titus 2:13-15*

WE STAND TODAY on the threshold of the most fantastic event in human history. It will be the most exciting and the most anticipated event that the world has ever known.

Nearly 2,000 years ago, Jesus Christ, God in human form, invaded human history. He walked among men for nearly thirty-three years. Then men nailed him to a cross. He didn't die because he was a sinner or because he deserved it, but because we needed forgiveness.

Before he returned to heaven, Jesus told his followers that one day toward the end of human history, when mankind was on the verge of destroying itself, when it was apparent man had failed, he would come back visibly, physically, literally to the earth.

It is this hope that Paul talked about now. "Looking for that blessed hope, and the glorious appearing of the great God and our Saviour Jesus Christ" (2:13). These verses point us toward the return of Jesus Christ. The first advent of Christ was prophesied throughout the Old Testament. His return, his second advent, is found throughout both the Old and New Testaments. It is the climax of human history. Jesus Christ is the climax of redemption, the culmination of history. Christ's return is central in God's Word. We speak much about grace and rightly believe that we are saved by grace through faith. Grace is mentioned 125 times in the New Testament. We speak about repentance and how repentance is necessary if a man is to see God. Repentance is mentioned seventy times in the New Testament. In the New Testament alone, the truth of the second coming of Christ is mentioned more than 380 times.

The fact that Jesus was born, lived, and died is history. The fact that he will come again is prophecy. Prophecy is just as sure as history. The only difference is that prophecy is history that God has seen before it takes place. We cannot undo the things in our past that we wish were erased from the record, and we cannot undo prophecy either. God is going to keep his word—Jesus Christ will surely return.

He came the first time to save man's soul. He will come the second time to save man's body. The body of the believer will be resurrected, redeemed, and glorified so that it is immortal. He came the first time to save the individual. He is coming again to save society. He came the first time to a crucifixion. He is coming a second time to a coronation, to a crown. He came the first time to a tree. He is coming the second time to a throne. He came the first time in humiliation. He is coming again in glory, power, and authority. He came the first time in love. He is coming the second time in wrath. He came the first time and was judged by men. He comes again to be the Judge of men. He came the first time to stand before

Pilate. When he comes again, Pilate will stand before him. The climax of human history and divine redemption will come when Jesus Christ comes again.

OUR POSITION

We are to be "looking for that blessed hope, even the glorious appearing of the great God and our Saviour Jesus Christ." We are to be looking for his return. "Looking" is an active verb which means "to give attention to something." We must not be asleep or caught off guard. We are to live in anticipation of the coming of Christ. We are to be ready for his return. To be "looking for" means to have a personal expectation, to be ready with a welcome for the person expected to come.

What a tragedy that so many people who know Jesus Christ give no thought to his return. Jesus said that we need to be on the lookout for his coming, for when we do not expect it he will come again (Matthew 24:42-44). He is coming as a thief in the night (1 Thessalonians 5:2). We must be vigilant, alert, expecting his return.

How can we be ready for his coming? By being sure that our lives are committed to the will of God. One may say, "I have plenty of time to be saved." But God declares that now is the time. "To-day if ye will hear his voice, harden not your hearts" (Hebrews 3:7, 8). If we are to be ready for the return of Christ, we must be obedient to him. After we have been saved, we must live in a vital relationship with him. Our sins must be confessed, so he can cleanse, direct, comfort, and strengthen our lives. That is the only way we can be ready.

Some people say, "I do not want him to come." If we feel that way, then we do not know him as we ought. When he comes again, it will be the perfect fulfillment of everything we dream for. Some families say, "We want our family to have more time together." In eternity, we will be with him, and relationships will be unmarred by the limitations of life. There will be no funeral services there. There will be no misunderstandings there, no communication gaps. There will be perfect relationship there. Our prayer should be, "Dear Lord, come quickly," for that which we delight in on this earth will be perfected when he comes again.

Our part is to be obedient to his will and open to his purposes. The Christian position is to be one of welcome and readiness for God to come. May we be looking for him, ministering, loving, sharing, helping each other, ready for his return.

OUR PROMISE

We are to be "looking for that blessed hope." The word "blessed" is translated several ways in the New Testament. It is sometimes translated "happy." His coming is a happy hope, a fond hope. Another meaning is "prosperous." The hope of Jesus Christ blesses and helps us. It puts meaning and purpose into our lives. It dissolves the despair that grips our souls so often.

"Hope" in the Bible is not something that we wish for, but something that we are assured will occur. We look forward to Christ's return because he has promised to come back.

Hope involves the future. We can't hope for something that has already happened. Nor do we hope for something that is bad. We hope for something that is desirable, something that is possible. Why hope for something that cannot happen? Christ's coming is going to take place in the future; it is desirable and it is possible for him to come. The second coming is not myth or wishful thinking, but a reality.

We are told by some that Christ cannot come now, that there are other things which must occur in the course of the divine plan of redemption before Jesus can return. But the Word of God very clearly says, "looking for [expecting, anticipating] that blessed hope."

The translation "looking for that blessed hope, and the glorious appearing" is unfortunate, because it seems to say that the hope is one thing and the glorious appearing is another. It should read, "looking for that glorious hope, even the glorious appearing of our great God." The next event on God's calendar is the glorious appearing of Jesus Christ.

Why is it necessary for him to return? Jesus must come again because of the helplessness of man. Man is sinful; he is far less than he ought to be. Through the years man has tried everything he can to lift the despair of human life, but he is still helpless, socially and individually. There has never been a time in human history when there were more wars than there are today. The prejudice, the hatred, the resentment and strife between men in society is stronger than ever. We have more knowledge than ever before, we have attained technological progress unthought of fifty years ago, we have put a man on the moon—but we do not know how to live with ourselves. We have conquered outer space, but we have not conquered inner space.

We are socially helpless in our world. This is the most affluent age the world has ever seen; yet we are afraid to leave our homes unlocked, walk down the street late at night, or leave our cars unlocked. Man is his own biggest problem. We need God.

How can mankind be delivered from this helplessness? God will send Christ back to earth to establish the peace, happiness, and fulfillment that man has failed to achieve.

The Word of God is filled with prophecy concerning the return of Jesus Christ. It is found in the Gospels, in the epistles, in the books of law, the books of history, the books of poetry and prophecy. One out of every twenty-five verses in the New Testament refers to the second coming of Christ. It is the hope of the Word of God.

The return of Jesus Christ will signal the day when the dominion of sin will be forever broken and conquered. I read with great emotion the story of the emancipation of slaves in the British West Indies. The night before they were to be declared free, they did not sleep. Down in the valleys in the West Indian villages, the people stayed up all night. Sentries were stationed on top of the mountains and hills surrounding the villages. The sentry's task was to herald the coming of dawn, for at sunrise they would be free. Those sentries on the hilltops would see the first rays of the sun even before the valley was aware of the light. Then the valleys resounded with the joyful sounds of deliverance.

Our hearts long for that day when we will be free from the burdens, the sadness, the disappointments, the disillusionments, and the depressions of this life. To be free is the hope of the heart. When Christ comes, that which is imperfect will be made perfect, that which is left undone will be complete. That is our hope.

Today the spirits of departed saints are with Christ, but their bodies are still in the grave. When Christ comes again, the bodies will be resurrected, glorified, and immortalized. Concerning this Jesus declared, "Neither can they die any more: for they are equal unto the angels; and are the children of God, being the children of the resurrection" (Luke 20:36). Heaven is empty of glorified bodies today, except for the body of Christ. But when Jesus comes again and the saints are raised and glorified, heaven will be populated with millions of saints. That is the hope of heaven, to be filled with those whose bodies cannot die.

Creation groans and labors under the curse of sin (Romans 8:21, 22). The oak tree grows, lifts its mighty boughs to heaven, decays, and dies. Men are born, men die. Flowers grow and bloom, and we rejoice in their beauty; but their leaves wither and die. Creation waits for the coming of Christ when the world will become new and eternal. His coming is the hope of creation.

When he comes, our redemption will be complete. The bodies of those who have died are in the earth. Our own bodies decay and if he tarries, we shall all walk through the valley of the shadow of death. But when he returns, the bodies of those who have gone before us will be raised and the living Christians will join them, and together we will be with him. Our redemption will be complete with his coming.

Sometimes it seems that good is penalized and evil is rewarded, that justice does not come. The record will be set straight when he comes. Then victory will be ours, righteousness will be vindicated.

When he returns, we shall stand individually face to face with our Lord. We rejoice when we hear someone sing about this. We shout in our hearts when we read in his Word about it. On that day, we shall stand face to face with him and shall be like him. That is the climax of our faith, the culmination of the ages. From before the foundation of the world, God saw his Son slain on the cross, raised up, and coming again.

Our task is to be ready. We are to be watching and hoping for his return. That means that each day we place our lives beside his revealed will and commit ourselves to it. Only then will his coming be the "blessed hope" it is intended to be for us.

 The Christian
in Society
*Titus 3:1-3*

"PUT THEM IN MIND to be subject to principalities and powers, to obey magistrates, to be ready to every good work, to speak evil of no man, to be no brawlers, but gentle, showing all meekness unto all men. For we ourselves also were sometime foolish, disobedient, deceived, serving divers lusts and pleasures, living in malice and envy, hateful, and hating one another" (3:1-3).

"Put them in mind" means "to call it to their attention, to cause them to remember it." We need to be reminded how we are to live. That is what the pastor-teacher is for. If we get uncomfortable or even angry at these admonitions, we need to remember that God has given us spiritual leaders to remind us of such things.

Here in America, we routinely elect governmental leaders. Other countries often have great difficulty having elections. We are told that we are to be subject to those who are in power, and yet we have the privilege of electing those to whom we will be subject. That is a rare privilege. We can help select those to whom we will give respect, honor, and obedience. Very few people in

the world have that opportunity. These verses tell us
something about our lives in relation to our society.


THE POWERS
On the island of Crete, the Christians were largely misunderstood. A new group, they were greeted with suspi-
cion by the ruling powers. They were such a small group
that they had little opportunity to change the direction of
their government. Yet even these Christians who were
mistreated, who did not get a fair shake, who were
oppressed were still told to be subject to those in authority. The same goes for us.

"Principalities" literally means "the first" or the
"leader," whoever is in the position of responsibility.
"Powers" refers to the system by which we are ruled.
We are to obey "magistrates," which speaks of anyone in
the position of authority; or more particularly, desig-
nated authority, anyone who is in a responsible position
in our society. That could be a policeman, a judge, a city
official, anyone who is in a position of leadership in a
community, elected or appointed.

Our responsibility is to be subject and to obey. Paul
defines this more clearly elsewhere. "Obey the government, for God is the one who has put it there. There is
no government anywhere that God has not placed in
power. So those who refuse to obey the laws of the land
are refusing to obey God, and punishment will follow.
For the policeman does not frighten people who are
doing right; but those doing evil will always fear him.

So if you don't want to be afraid, keep the laws and you will get along well. The policeman is sent by God to help you. But if you are doing something wrong, of course you should be afraid, for he will have you punished. He is sent by God for that very purpose" (Romans 13:1-4, TLB). This very plainly declares that civil authorities have the right to uphold the law. We need to understand that and view them as those "sent by God," who are to minister to us in the best interests of our society.

There is no justification for a child of God to be disrespectful of those in a position of leadership. We may not like all the things that they do, we may not approve of all the things they choose to present, but they are ministers of God. We are to uphold them with our prayers and be obedient to the law of the land. The Christian should be the best citizen anywhere, living his life in such a way that he encourages and helps society.

There should be no question on which side of the law the Christian stands. There are only three occasions given in the Word of God where a Christian is justified in breaking the law. First, when it interferes with our prayer life, as in the king's decree in the time of Daniel (Daniel 6:4-9). If the law were to say we cannot pray, we obviously could not obey. Secondly, if it were to interfere with our worship as it did with the three Hebrew children who were thrown into the fiery furnace (Daniel 3:8-18), we could not obey the law. Thirdly, if it interferes with our witness, as it did in the early church (Acts 5:28), we must obey God.

But as long as the law of the land does not violate a principle of my relationship with God, my position is to be obedient, to live within the framework of the law. So let it be known, once and for all, that we as God's children stand by the side of law and law enforcement, and by the side of those who are given the responsibility under God to uphold that law.

We are also "to be ready to every good work." We are to be a healthy part of community life, a part of things that are wholesome and helpful in our communities. Christians ought to be involved in the political and social processes at work around them. We should work for the improvement of our community. We should encourage good things to happen and be interested in raising the level of life for those in need.

The reason our communities have the problems they have is because most citizens do not want to be involved. The Word of God tells us that we must do what we can to help people and communities to be what they ought to be. As Christians, we must take a stand, we must be involved—God has given us that responsibility.

THE PEOPLE

What is our relationship to be to each other in the community (verse 2)? He is not just speaking of those within the church fellowship, though everything said here certainly should be true of the fellowship of the church as well.

We are "to speak evil of no man." We must slander no one. A Christian is not to spread bad news about other people. He is not to say things that are not in the best interest of those involved. In our society, often the only test we use is, Is it true? The Christian can never make that the only test of what he says. Some things are true, but are also hurtful. The test of whether or not something should be said is, Is it helpful? Or will it slander the name of another or bring hurt to the community and to the people in it?

Further, the Christian must not be a gossip. He must not deliberately say things that are not true. We are to be part of the solution and not the problem, part of the healing and not the hurt, part of the blessing and not the disease in society. We are not to give opportunity for that spirit within each of us that wants to reveal the worst that we know about others to gain at their expense. We are to be very careful about what we say, not only within the fellowship of the church, but also in the community.

One of the problems within the church is that we have "super-Christians" who look down on everyone else. No one else is as gifted, or as true to the Word, or as "spiritual." Christians should beware of such an attitude.

This does not mean that we shouldn't take a stand against evil, but it means that we should not maliciously spread "news" about individuals that is harmful and poisonous. We are to carefully guard our speech.

Furthermore, we are "to be no brawlers." That word means "abstaining from fighting and contentiousness." This is not speaking of physical violence, but arguing, debating, and divisiveness. The Christian should not be looking for an argument. I am disappointed when I see great segments of the Christian community thriving on condemnation. They take the Bible and beat others to death with it. This is not the spirit of Christ. We are not looking for a fight. We are also to be "gentle," a word meaning "to be kind and gracious." Kindness should be the pattern of our lives toward others.

We are also to be "showing all meekness unto all men." That literally means that we allow people who are outside the faith to mistreat us without retaliating, because we know God is still in control. We are to be meek toward those who might take advantage of us, those who might say false things about us. We are to take it humbly and graciously because we recognize the hand of God in purifying and maturing our own faith. We are to be completely meek "unto all men," not only those in the faith.

THE PAST
We need to remember what we used to be (verse 3). Most of us have forgotten what it was like to be lost. This passage reminds us. The reason we can be kind toward the unbeliever, and be gentle and meek, is because we ourselves were at one time rebels against God, wandering in darkness because we believed Satan's lies.

"For we ourselves also were sometime foolish." The word "foolish" means "without intelligence." Because there is no real intelligence apart from God, before we came to God we were fools. Our own intelligence was worthless without the Spirit of God enlarging our minds and opening to us the whole world of spiritual reality and spiritual truth.

We were "disobedient," a word referring to one who refuses to be persuaded. We deliberately refused to believe the truth. We did not want to be children of God. We wanted to do our own thing. We refused to respond to God.

We were "deceived." The Spirit of God was unable to bring spiritual truth to our lives because we were blinded by Satan (1 Corinthians 2:12-14). Satan kept us from the things that were real, the things that were true. Our hearts and minds were closed to God and deceived.

We were "serving divers lusts and pleasures" through various appetites of the human body. We were slaves to our passions, to our own appetites. We could not control our lust, our greed, our ambition. We were at the mercy of those passions. The man who serves his passions is always at the mercy of his own insecurities and inconsistencies. We were once like that, doing whatever seemed natural, and always coming up frustrated and empty.

Further, we were "living in malice and envy." Malice involves wrong attitudes toward others. The best synonym for malice is malignancy. We had a spiteful, hurtful, destructive attitude toward others. We were envious of everyone who had more than we did.

We were "hateful, and hating one another." We hated ourselves and everybody else. That is the way we used to be.

"But after that the kindness and love of God our

Saviour toward man appeared" (3:4). After our foolishness and rebellion against God, the kindness and love of God our Savior appeared. For it was "not by works of righteousness which we have done, but according to his mercy he saved us, by the washing of regeneration, and renewing of the Holy Ghost" (3:5).

We can never be the citizens we should be by ourselves. We can never have the right kind of attitudes toward our neighbors and fellowmen by ourselves. By ourselves we are everything that was described in verse 3. But Jesus came into our hearts, and everything that we could never become he made us to be. Everything that we desperately needed but could never produce in our selves, he brought into our lives. Not because of our works or any goodness that we did, but according to his grace and his mercy he saved us. He gave us his Holy Spirit to live in our hearts, so that everything that our society needs us to be, we can become.

There has never been a time in the history of our republic when we needed good citizens as much as today. The only alternative to obedience to civil authority is anarchy and chaos. We are moving rapidly toward that time. The turmoil occurring around the world will happen to us unless there is a new breed of citizen, a citizen who does not think about himself first. There is a need for statesmen who can change the course of a nation. There is a need for new leadership, and a need for new citizens. The only way we can be the leaders we ought to be and the citizens we ought to be is through Jesus Christ, by his grace coming into our hearts.

We thank God for what he has done. We praise God

for the opportunities he has given to us. Let us bow our knees and claim him first as Savior, then obey him as Lord. Then we will be to the powers and to the people what we ought to be. We will not live as we did in the past. There will be new people making a new society through the presence of the Holy Spirit in their hearts.

## Man's Best Is Not Enough
### Titus 3:4-7

IN THESE VERSES we have one of the clearest statements of the Christian faith anywhere in the Bible, the message of how a person is saved, how one may have the power to face life and its challenge. The words are very carefully and deliberately chosen. "But after that the kindness and love of God our Saviour toward man appeared, not by works of righteousness which we have done, but according to his mercy he saved us, by the washing of regeneration, and renewing of the Holy Ghost; which he shed on us abundantly through Jesus Christ our Saviour; that being justified by his grace, we should be made heirs according to the hope of eternal life" (3:4-7).

As we have already seen, the verses just before this describe what the Christians at Crete used to be, before they met Christ. One word in those verses serves as an introduction to the verses we'll look at now—the word "deceive." A person who has been deceived has been made to look like a fool. He is living a pipe dream and he will have to pay the piper before it is all over. Satan uses deception as one of his main tools.

Many people today think that salvation comes by their

own efforts. They believe that if a man works hard enough, he'll find some sort of utopia, some kind of salvation. We will see in this passage that this is a false hope.

Paul is declaring that there is only one way for a person to be a whole person. Apart from this, man is on a merry-go-round seeking new thrills, new highs, but always finds himself depressed and defeated. The whole person is one for whom God has brought all the pieces together. Only God can rebuild Humpty Dumpty lives. Only God can put a human life, shattered by deception, back together.

THE MANIFESTATION

Despite all our deception, "the kindness and love of God our Saviour toward man appeared" (3:4). This is one of the most interesting combinations of attributes describing God that we will ever find. "Kindness," often attributed to God, literally means "benign." God does not want to hurt us. His interest in us is covered in kindness. He wants us to find fulfillment and happiness.

God's love for us appeared in the person of Jesus Christ. If we desire to know what God's attitude toward us is, we have but to look at Jesus. Everything Jesus Christ endured, every pain, every moment of hatred, every sacrifice was because of God's great desire to help us.

"The love of God our Saviour has appeared." The word for "love" is significant here. It is not *agape* but *phileo*. It means that God loves man because man is human. This word is the source of our English word "philanthropy." God has a genuine love for man as he created him. He wants us to be perfectly human. He loves man because of what man as a human being can become. There is hope for mankind because man is God's creation.

This is not to say that God does not love us on a higher level, the *agape* level. The emphasis here is that God loves us as human beings. None of us are the kind of people we ought to be. God loves us anyway. God cares about us in spite of our rebellion and sin.

Verse 4 says that God is our Savior. Verse six calls Jesus Christ our Savior. The Word of God continually speaks about God and Christ with the same reverence. They are one and the same. God is our Savior. Christ is our Savior. Jesus said, "I and my Father are one" (John 10:30). We must always keep prominent in our hearts the fact that Jesus Christ is fully the Son of God. He is fully divine. He is God.

Many false doctrines in the world today pull Jesus Christ down to a human level. Any teaching that robs him of his deity must be rejected quickly. Jesus Christ is God's Son. He existed in the beginning with God. He is the very essence of God. He is the expressed image of God.

THE MIRACLE
"Not by works of righteousness which we have done, but according to his mercy he saved us. . . ." (3:5). The only way a man ever comes to be saved is through what God does. There is not any work of righteousness we can

do. We are saved by his works of righteousness—his mercy and his grace. We are saved by his works, not ours. We are not saved because of an agreement between God and us, but because of an agreement between the Father and Christ. God provides salvation. My part is to simply receive it.

The works of righteousness spoken of here are those works revealed in the Old Testament. It would not, however, have to be confined to those. Any good thing we are able to do is a work of righteousness. But we cannot earn salvation. For example, we cannot be baptized to be saved. Baptism is very important to the Christian, but it's not baptism that makes him a Christian. We are baptized not because we want to be saved, but because we have been saved and want to be obedient to Christ.

The word "saved" is in the past perfect tense, meaning that it has been done and cannot be undone or redone. It is complete. It is a fact established by his grace and by his mercy. This salvation is not something we can change or lose. It is not dependent upon what we keep on doing. Salvation was accomplished in the past and stands complete in the present. That's the miracle of salvation.

Paul continued with the phrase, "by the washing of regeneration." Some think this refers to baptism. However, these verses are speaking of salvation from God's viewpoint. God does the washing. "The washing of regeneration" refers to sins being washed away.

Look at some biblical examples. David, centuries before Christ ever came and before there would be any understanding of baptism as we know it, declared, "Wash me thoroughly from mine iniquity, and cleanse me from my sin" (Psalm 51:2). Obviously David was not speaking about water baptism. He was describing an experience of cleansing by God's Holy Spirit.

Zechariah, the prophet, described a fountain of cleansing (13:1) that would be opened to the people of God, washing them from their sins. Obviously, he did not have in mind baptism, because it was not understood then as it is today.

In Ephesians 5, when Paul was telling us how husbands ought to love their wives, he told them to love their wives even "as Christ also loved the church, and gave himself for it; that he might sanctify it and cleanse it with the washing of water by the word" (Ephesians 5:25, 26). That is the same washing that Paul was talking about in Titus.

In Revelation, we read of those who "came out of great tribulation, and have washed their robes, and made them white in the blood of the Lamb" (Revelation 7:14). In the Word of God, washing and cleansing come through the blood of Christ. When we give our hearts to Christ, he takes our sins and plunges them under his blood, and so unites us with himself. We become his peculiar, unique possession. That is the washing of regeneration.

Paul further spoke of "the renewing of the Holy Ghost" (3:5). "Renewing" comes from two words meaning "new" and "again," an obvious reference to the new birth. We are born again when the Holy Spirit of God comes into our lives. Paul continued, "Which he shed on us abundantly through Jesus Christ our Saviour" (3:6). God does not give us just enough to get saved. Salvation is more than an escape from hell. God has given us the Holy Spirit "abundantly," richly, fully. When we become children of God, he plants his Holy Spirit in us and through him keeps giving us glory, victory, power, abundant life.

God saves us from our sins and then places himself in us so that we will be taught how not to sin. When we become Christians, God doesn't lose his interest in us. He just redirects his interest in us. Before, he was concerned that we would be saved. Now he is concerned that we be sanctified, that we learn to walk the Christian life.

Throughout the book of Titus, there is the tremendous emphasis that if we are Christians we should live like it. There ought to be something different about us. Unsaved people should be able to see God in our lives. God saves us and then keeps pouring out his Spirit richly on us so we can be his displays in this world.

Paul then described us as "being justified" (3:7). When we are saved, we are judged righteous once and for all. It does not have to be redone; it cannot be undone. We become "heirs" of eternal life. In this world, things are imperfect, we are imperfect. We are incapable of allowing God the full liberty he desires in our lives. But in a coming day, Christ will come again, and we will be heirs with him. We will inherit God's eternal riches. We will become like Christ fully and completely.

What we have now is a down payment, an "earnest" (2 Corinthians 1:22) of our inheritance, a foretaste of eternity. It is sweet now, but it will get infinitely better. Each day we walk with Christ *is* sweeter than the day before. Circumstances may change. Physical comforts may disappear. The affection of friends may weaken. Financial security may totter. All these things may fail, but God is faithful. Through God there is a continual progress toward that day when we shall receive our inheritance.

This passage reminds us that salvation is entirely in God's hands. We are not saved because we feel funny, bubbly, nervous, or excited. We are saved because God loved us. When we give our hearts to him, he comes into our lives. That's a fact! Thus we receive salvation and become heirs of life with him.

How tragic if one joins the church, thinking that's all he needs. How sad if someone considers himself acceptable to God because he has performed man's religious rituals. Man's righteousness is wasted effort. The works that God wants us to do are not to save us, but to express our salvation and share it with those around us. God's works secure our salvation.

Keep Living
Right
*Titus 3:8-11*

THIS PASSAGE is virtually a summary of the entire book of Titus. God has to make a continual reemphasis upon basic truths or else we will let them slip. The repeated emphasis of the book of Titus is that a Christian ought to act like a Christian. The child of God should be a consistent witness for Christ.

"This is a faithful saying, and these things I will that thou affirm constantly, that they which have believed in God might be careful to maintain good works. These things are good and profitable unto men. But avoid foolish questions, and genealogies, and contentions, and strivings about the law; for they are unprofitable and vain. A man that is a heretic after the first and second admonition, reject; knowing that he that is such is subverted, and sinneth, being condemned of himself" (3:8-11).

The word "faithful" comes from a root word very commonly translated "faith." In the third verse of the first chapter, it is translated "committed." Real faith involves both trust and commitment. It is not simply a matter of believing something to be so intellectually, but also of

Keep Living
Right

trusting and committing. These two aspects of faith go
hand in hand.

The word translated "saying" is a very common word,
*largos*, simply referring to what has been spoken. Paul
was declaring that the word we have heard, the gospel
we have received, is worthy of our trust and commitment. We can believe in these things.

This passage has to do with those "which have believed in God." It is written to those who believe in God,
who have begun the venture of faith. This advice and this
counsel are addressed to us.

AN AFFIRMATION
"These things I will that thou affirm constantly, that
they which have believed in God might be careful to
maintain good works. These things are good and profitable unto men." We are to affirm certain things "constantly." That word does not mean continually, but consistently, with the same zest, same enthusiasm, in the
same basic manner.

In Crete there were Judaizers who claimed to be Christians, but also kept the Old Testament regulations and
laws. They taught that the Gentiles had to be circumcised, that Christians had to adhere to all the old forms
of Jewish ceremonial cleanliness and ritual. This would
enslave believers to the old Jewish system. These men
were positively affirming falsehood.

If one enthusiastically proclaims erroneous doctrine,
he doesn't make it true just by being enthusiastic about

it, even if he convinces us that it's true. Paul was telling Titus that the true believer should have just as much zest and enthusiasm for the truth. We should explode with the truth of the gospel. We are to express God's truth with all of our energy and all of our heart wherever we are. We are enthusiastic about so many things, yet seem hesitant and bashful about the gospel. We need to give that same natural enthusiasm to the teaching and sharing of the Word of God. We are to continually, uniformly, consistently affirm that which we have heard. We must let the truth roll from our hearts and mouths and let it be seen in our lives.

Why is consistent affirmation so important? So that Christians will "be careful to maintain good works." Here again is the emphasis on living what we say we believe. Being "careful" means to give consideration to, to study, to give serious thought to, to give great diligence to. The word "maintain" literally means "to stand in front of."

Let me illustrate it this way. In many foreign countries, merchants stand in front of their stores and try to persuade customers to come inside and buy merchandise. That is what this word meant. There are two possible meanings to the word "maintain," a vocational word. It could mean that a Christian ought to have a godly and useful vocation, one that honors God. Whatever we do to make a living ought to bring glory to God. That is one of the meanings.

But probably the strongest explanation of this phrase is that we are to live our lives in such a way that we are useful and helpful to other people. The phrase, "these things are good and profitable unto men," means that we Christians need to affirm the gospel so positively and so completely with all our hearts that we demonstrate a useful and helpful life that is good and encouraging to others. How wonderful it would be if we would do that for each other—if we would lift each other's spirits, care for each other, be useful and helpful to one another. That is the kind of lives we are to live.

We are also to "avoid foolish questions, and genealogies, and contentions, and strivings about the law; for they are unprofitable and vain" (3:9). The word "foolish" is *moros*. We get our word "moron" from it. "How many angels can sit on the head of a pin?" We are to avoid foolish questions that have no bearing on life.

Further, we are to avoid genealogies. One of the Jews' favorite studies was to trace their ancestors back and see if they came from the "right" line. It does not really matter what our earthly lineage is, or what our background may be. We do not go to heaven or gain spiritual maturity because of our background, but on the basis of our own personal faith in Jesus Christ.

We are to avoid "contentions." This could be translated "strife." It never honors God when his people argue among themselves.

Then too, we are to avoid "strivings about the law." The Pharisees' favorite pastime seemed to be to think up new ways to interpret or apply the Old Testament law. They had many requirements for things they were to do and not to do, adding literally hundreds of man-made traditions to the commands of Scripture.

In our day we sometimes practice the same kind of

legalism. Tithing is a good example. Many of us seem to think that once we have given ten percent, we have done everything God has asked. Ten percent belongs to God, but then again everything belongs to God. God may ask us to give ten percent, or thirty percent, or fifty percent. The tithe is a guideline, not something to be legalistic about.

Arguments about the law are "unprofitable." No one ever grows through them. They don't lead to maturity or progress. Legalists are just treading water, not going forward in the Christian life.

Such arguments are also "vain" or fruitless. No one ever gets saved as a result of them. Theological debates do not help the Christian mature or draw lost men to God.

Now we are told to reject a person who is a heretic, a person who perverts spiritual truth. The heretic is contentious, critical, and schismatic. We are to warn him once, then twice, and after that leave him alone.

Certainly we are to endeavor to be reconciled with others. But we reach a point where, according to the Scripture, we are to leave them alone. God reminds us that there are a lot of people hungry for the Word; so move on to them. Don't get bogged down with the hard-hearted.

AN ACCUSATION

Notice the arraignment or accusation in verse 11. The reason we should leave the heretic alone is clear: "Knowing that he that is such is subverted, and sinneth, being condemned of himself."

The heretic is "subverted," or twisted inside out. He is so warped and twisted in his mind and heart that it is useless to reason with him or try to counsel him. He doesn't want to hear. He "sinneth"; that is, he is wicked and rebellious against God's purposes. Third, he is "being condemned of himself." The contentious person, the schismatic, always factious, always trying to bring disharmony, is his own worst enemy. If we give him enough rope, he will hang himself.

This paragraph of Titus started with "This is a faithful saying." We can confidently commit ourselves to the ways and purposes of God. We must not be dragged into contentions, strife, and disharmony. Rather, we are to move forward, serving God in a manner that is encouraging and helpful to those around us.

The Blessed
Bond of Love
*Titus 3:12-15*

THIS IS OBVIOUSLY the "yours truly" of Paul's letter to
Titus. The churches on Crete, where Titus was serving,
had faced oppression by unbelievers and infiltration by
false teachers. Now Paul closed his letter with some very
personal, practical matters.

"When I shall send Artemas unto thee, or Tychicus,
be diligent to come unto me to Nicopolis: for I have
determined there to winter. Bring Zenas the lawyer and
Apollos on their journey diligently, that nothing be
wanting unto them. And let ours also learn to maintain
good works for necessary uses, that they be not unfruitful. All that are with me salute thee. Greet them that
love us in the faith. Grace be with you all. Amen"
(3:12-15).

The Apostle Paul planned to spend the winter in Nicopolis and was sending this message by Artemas or
Tychicus. Titus was to meet him in Nicopolis and provide
for his needs there. It is obvious that Paul's friendship
with Titus went very deep.

Paul mentioned Zenas the lawyer, the only time a
lawyer is mentioned by name in the Bible. There may

have been some legal things required and Zenas ministered to Paul in that way, just as Luke the physician
ministered to him medically. Apollos, also to be brought
to Nicopolis, was a bright young preacher and teacher.

We may look at this paragraph and feel it has very little
to do with us today. However, there are three very significant and practical things in these verses for us.

GRATITUDE

"Bring Zenas the lawyer and Apollos on their journey
diligently, that nothing be wanting unto them" (3:13).
Zenas and Apollos were about to take a journey in the
name of the Lord and the church, perhaps leaving their
living behind. The Apostle Paul was saying, "You Christians in Crete be sure to send them on their journey
lacking nothing." Their gratitude to God for the ministry
of these men would lead them to make provision for
them.

In God's Word there is strong emphasis upon taking
care of those who give us spiritual leadership. We cannot
even casually read through the New Testament without
being aware of this responsibility. In fact, we are told
that we should take care of those who minister to us out
of gratitude to God. It is God who has called them, sent
them out, given them a message, and helped them
minister to our hearts.

In 1 Timothy 5:18, Paul quotes Leviticus 19:13 and
Deuteronomy 24:15—"the laborer is worthy of his re-
ward." We should provide for the ones who minister

to us graciously and joyfully. God has ministered to us through others! Now we have many opportunities to provide for their needs, and we are to do it gladly from our hearts. We are not to force them to be beggars. It is our privilege to provide for their needs.

GENEROSITY

"And let ours also learn to maintain good works for necessary uses." Paul was simply declaring that we need to work very hard to pay our bills, but also to have enough to help someone else. This is the grace of generosity, the spirit that should be seen among the people of God so they can minister to those in need. We ought to maintain good works that are healthy, wholesome, and encouraging.

"Continue to love each other with true brotherly love. Don't forget to be kind to strangers, for some who have done this have entertained angels without realizing it! Don't forget about those in jail. Suffer with them as though you were there yourself. Share the sorrow of those being mistreated, for you know what they are going through" (Hebrews 13:1-3, TLB).

We are to have compassion for one another. We are to develop the grace of generosity and hospitality. Earlier Paul declared that the bishop is to be a lover of hospitality. We can tell a lot about our Christianity by how generous and gracious we are. Do we willingly share what God has entrusted to us?

This does not mean that the church is to become a

social welfare agency. But there should be no Christian beggars. The churches in the first century were instructed to provide for the needs of the saints. When a Christian was hungry, they fed him. When a believer had no place to stay, they opened their homes to him. When a brother or sister had a need, they ministered to that need. Somehow we have lost something of that in our day. We must learn to make provision for each other's needs. If we are generous, our works will not be unfruitful but will bear gracious, mature fruit.

GRACE
The last word of this epistle is the word for "grace." God's wonderful, saving, and sustaining grace. The grace of God was an amazement to Paul as he looked at his own life and considered that he was chief among all sinners. Yet God in his grace saved him and called him to preach the unsearchable riches of salvation.

God never chooses any of us except by his grace. No man preaches because he is good, effective, or talented. He preaches by the grace of God. None of us serves in a position of responsibility in the church or assumes a place of spiritual responsibility because we are talented or deserving, but because of the grace of God. We are saved and we serve by the grace of God.

Paul said three things in this final verse. "All that are with me salute thee." That means to wish well, to say "God bless you," "go with God," "we are wishing you well and praying for you." It was this spirit of greeting that they sent. It is a warm spirit of prayer that is suspended from the heart of one group of people to the heart of another. We should build that kind of spirit among God's people. We are so competitive among the churches of our communities that we lose sight of such gracious, compassionate concern for the welfare of others.

We are to "greet them that love us in the faith." Most of us would be impossible to love any other way. We are just not lovely or lovable. But in the faith there is love, a love that transcends barriers. The love of God binds our hearts together.

God's love bridges generation gaps. There are no young and old in Christ; all ages are one. God's love bridges racial barriers. There is no black, brown, white, red, or yellow in Christ. All races are one in Christ.

The world desperately longs to observe God's people loving each other as they should. The tie that binds our hearts together is an indescribable blessing and delight in the faith.

Paul concluded by saying, "Grace be with you all." God's sustaining, ever-powerful grace is what we need. The deeper the valley we walk, the more the grace of God is poured out on us. As we greet each other in love, God's grace will be with us.